SPIRITUAL JOURNAL

by
Dr. Billie Hanks, Jr.
with
Billy Beacham

The full SPIRITUAL JOURNAL is a unique book, a notebook and a devotional guide which lasts a year*, and may be started at any time.

In his Introduction, Billie Hanks writes of the difference a Quiet Time made in his own life, and says, 'When the Lord opens a passage in the Bible to your understanding or teaches you some important lesson through the living of life, you are being entrusted with a pearl of great worth.'

The SPIRITUAL JOURNAL will give you the opportunity to meditate on what God is teaching you. It begins with a *Quiet Time Section* with space for writing down Scriptural insights and prayers for each day of the year. Then follows a *Note Taking Section* and an *Additional Aids Section*, which includes a Bible reading plan.

Printed on high grade paper, SPIRITUAL JOURNAL, published by Word UK, may be obtained from your local Christian Bookshop.

*UK edition. Quarterly edition available in USA.

If You Love Me

1
The Love of God

But as many as received Him, to them He gave the right to become the children of God, even to those who believe in His name. (John 1:12)

The depth of God's love for us is revealed in the fact that He wants us to become His very own children. Everyone in the world was created by God, and each one of us shares the same heavenly invitation to become far more than His creation. God wants us to be His children, members of His family.

To explain this invitation, the Bible focuses on two important words of action: *believe* and *receive.* Pretend you have a glass of water in your hand. You are hot and thirsty and nearly dehydrated. You believe the water is cool and good and sweet, but it cannot quench your thirst until you drink it—until your parched body *receives* it. Believing without receiving is not enough! Believing is only the beginning.

God designed our physical bodies to need water, and He uniquely created water to meet that physical need. The spiritual principle of life is exactly the same. We needed to know God, and God sent His Son, Jesus Christ, into the world to meet that spiritual need. When we receive Christ into our hearts, we come to know our heavenly Father. Through this unique relationship He provides all the love, forgiveness, and guidance we will ever need. He quenches our thirst for His presence. His well will never run dry.

Another parallel between physical reality and spiritual reality can be seen in architecture. No superstructure is ever built without first laying a foundation. This is universally true. In 1 Corinthians 3:11, Paul says, ". . . no man can lay a foundation other than the one which is laid, which is Jesus Christ." You must believe enough in the Lord's power to change you to receive Him by faith and let Him establish that spiritual foundation in your life.

Beginning a New Life

Years ago, in Anchorage, Alaska, I taught a conference on spiritual growth. A young woman who had attended every session seemed to be unhappy; there was no radiance in her smile. She didn't laugh when others laughed, or take part in the activities. Toward the close of the week, as I taught on salvation, she began to cry. After the service she made her way to the front of the auditorium. I asked if she understood what I had been saying. She said that she had not understood anything for four nights, but that when John 1:12 on *believing* and *receiving* was explained, she saw her spiritual condition.

I explained that once we *realize* our need for forgiveness, there are two steps to salvation. The first is intellectual acceptance. The second is willingness to receive Christ by faith. I said, "He is a gentleman and will not force His way into your life. He knocks and wants to come in, but you must offer the invitation." She had never understood this before.

Residing in an apartment about three blocks from the church but never attending services, she had been living in adultery with a man for a long time. The week before, he had left a note simply saying, "I'm leaving. You'll never see me again." At the age of 23, she had a baby but no marriage, a past but no future, a present but no happiness. After reading the note she threw herself on the bed and prayed, "O God, I haven't talked to You for years, but if You are there, if You are real, please answer me. I have made a terrible mess of my life and I need Your help. I need forgiveness. I want to live differently."

Here was a young woman who had been to church not more than three times in her entire life. She had no relationship with Christ but was now sincerely seeking Him. In the quiet of her heart God impressed her to leave her apartment and enter the first church she saw. He let her know that the help she needed was waiting there. That was where we were conducting a city-wide conference on spiritual growth.

Arriving at the church, she saw books and a registration table. She paid the conference fee, thinking that must be the cost for going to church. Because everyone assumed that she was a member of a congregation other than their own, no one suspected her need. But she persevered in coming even though she sat alone every night.

On the fourth evening I went through the plan of salvation, illustrating how we were created by God but had been separated from Him by sin. I explained the wonderful news: that through believing in Christ and receiving Him, one could become a child of God. As the Holy Spirit opened her eyes, for the first time in her life she saw the importance of receiving Christ.

Her new life began with a prayer like this: "Lord, I believe in You and want You to be my Savior. Please come into my heart and take control of my life. I have sinned and need Your love and forgiveness." Her overwhelming joy was evident as she gave thanks that her prayer had been answered. Through the Lord Jesus Christ she was born into God's kingdom and became one of His very own children.

Today, many people do not understand that intellectual belief in God is not enough. They are surprised to learn that the Scriptures say that even the demons believe in one God, but that doesn't get them into heaven. Personal commitment is required for salvation. That is why the act of *receiving* Christ is so important.

Living with Assurance

After laying the spiritual foundation of *believing* and *receiving,* what comes next? In 1 John 5:13, the Bible says, "These things have I written unto you who believe upon the name of the Son of God in order that you may *know* that you have eternal life." The word "know" stands out as the emphasis of this verse. As

His children, God wants us to be assured of His love, faithfulness, and supreme adequacy to see us through both this life and the next. In His love He chose to let us *know* rather than guess or only hope about the reality of our salvation. God does not intend for us to wait until we die to find out if we are going to heaven. First John was written so that God's children might have that certainty.

In Romans 8:16, the apostle Paul says, "And the Spirit Himself bears witness with our spirit that we are children of God." It is God who reminds you that you are His child. With each passing year your assurance and understanding of that reality will grow. Though remembering the exact hour or day when you received Christ is desirable, it is not necessary. However, knowing that there was such a time is essential. Billy Graham's wife, Ruth, reared on the mission field in China, came to faith at an early age. When asked about her conversion, she once replied, "I don't know when the sun came up, but I'm sure it's shining." This certainty is the birthright of every person who receives Christ into his life.

I well remember my own conversion. I was only ten years old and alone in my room. Though I vividly recall making the decision, I cannot remember the date. But I will never forget the joy that filled my heart when I awakened my parents and said, "Mother and Dad, I have become a Christian." I knew what had happened! Although I had only prayed the single word, "yes," God knew all that implied. In later years, I have often thought of the simple prayer of the repentant thief on the cross who said, "Lord, remember me when You come into Your kingdom." [1] That was not a wordy request, but it was enough to make the difference in his eternal destiny, because God knew he meant it.

The Lord looks into our hearts. What we mean by what we say is far more important to Him than the way we say it. The sincere prayer of the smallest child is as pleasing and acceptable to Him as the petition of the most mature adult. If you have the inner peace that comes from knowing that you have sincerely invited Christ into your heart, reading the pages that follow can significantly deepen the quality of your relationship with Him.

However, if your life still has no spiritual foundation and you lack the assurance that you have received Christ into your life, you have *nothing to fear.* God has promised to honor the desires of your heart.[2] Though you may have believed in Christ with your mind since childhood, if you now realize your need to personally *receive* Him into your life, He is prepared to answer your petition.

Prayers of sincere repentance based upon Jesus' famous parable about the prodigal son [3] have been expressed to God by millions across the centuries. At the bottom of this page is a prayer that expresses what the Lord taught in that parable. If you feel the need to be certain of your own relationship with Christ, pray this prayer in faith.

There is no magic in the particular words of the Sinner's Prayer, for receiving Christ is an act of the *will.* Your prayer simply reflects the inward decision you are making. Have you trusted Christ completely for forgiveness and guidance? If not, these moments of earnest commitment will make the difference in how and where you spend eternity.

If you have been *hoping* that you are a Christian but want to know for *certain,* God wants you to have that *assurance.* Why not pause right now and quietly talk with Him? Consider each thought in this prayer, and express it to God in your own personal way.

SINNER'S PRAYER

"Lord Jesus, I am a sinner. But I am sorry for my sins. I want to turn from my sins and begin a new quality of life with Your help. Please come into my heart and take control of my life today. From this moment forward, my life belongs to You and You alone. I will love You, serve You, tell others about You, and trust You to live Your victorious life through me. Thank You, Lord, for coming into my life and forgiving my sins today."

What have you just done? You have acknowledged that the Lord Jesus Christ is your personal Savior! Because of this there is great *joy* in heaven. You might be saying to yourself, "This is wonderful! But what should I do next?" For salvation you have made the all-important step of receiving Christ by faith. Now you must learn how to walk in Him.

2
Learning to Walk

As you therefore have received Christ Jesus the Lord, so walk in Him. (Colossians 2:6)

Learning how to *walk* in Christ is your next step in Christian growth. In this step, you will discover the joy of telling others about your decision to follow Christ. The Lord said, "Whoever acknowledges me before men, I will also acknowledge him before my Father in heaven." [1] What does that mean? Simply this: When you love someone, it is natural to talk about them. You want others to know about the close friendship you share. The Lord wants no secret disciples, and when you love Him you will want to be baptized, join a church fellowship, and begin to witness where you work or go to school. These things will come naturally as you grow.

Before a person learns how to walk, he must learn to crawl. Walking and maturing are part of a process. There is no single moment when you suddenly become mature. It is the same in your spiritual pilgrimage: birth (receiving Christ) comes first. Then comes crawling, walking, and finally running. This involves wonderful years of growing in fellowship with God. The apostle Paul speaks of Christian maturity as running the race and finishing the course. [2]

Walking requires energy, and just as we gain physical strength through eating, we need to nourish ourselves spiritually. In 1 Peter 2:2 the apostle Paul says, "Like newborn babes, long for the pure milk of the word, that by it you may grow. . . ." When you were born, the first thing you needed was nourishment. A child needs milk. You don't have to instruct him to want it—the desire is natural. There is an excitement and beautiful satisfaction when that need is met. On a spiritual level, the desire to know God's Word corresponds to a baby's natural hunger. For this reason, the Word of God is often referred to as spiritual food.

How do you feed yourself spiritually, as you learn to walk in Christ? God has equipped us with five senses. One of these senses is the ability to hear. The Bible says, "Faith comes from what is preached, and what is preached comes from the word of Christ." [3] Every time you attend Sunday school or go to church, you have the opportunity to hear the Word of God. Each time you listen, you are given new spiritual truths. This is God's way of increasing our faith. Jesus said, ". . . Man shall not live by bread alone, but by every word that proceeds from the mouth of God." [4]

Listening is a primary means of spiritual growth; however, there is a fundamental hurdle which we must all overcome. Scientists have proven that we forget approximately 90 to 95 percent of what we hear after 72 hours. If you heard your favorite preacher or could even listen to the apostle Paul, you would still forget about 90 percent after three days. The truth is that most of us cannot remember much from last Sunday's sermon. This is not because of a lack of dedication. Our problem is retention! Unless what we hear meets a very specific need in our lives, we simply cannot remember it.

So notetaking is important. It compensates for our human tendency to forget; it encourages those who preach and teach from the Scriptures; and it helps us meditate on what we hear, so we can apply God's Word in our lives.

I discovered the value of notetaking after several years of frustration. As a teenager, I publicly rededicated my life nine times. The people at our church must have thought my life was filled with problems. In reality, however, my desire was simply to grow deeper in my commitment to Christ. It was not that I had become less dedicated. I simply didn't know how to retain the blessings

I was receiving. Unfortunately, there was no place on the commitment card which said, "I want to be a man or woman whom God can use, and I need someone to teach me."

Perhaps you have had a similar experience. If so, learning how to listen will be essential to your spiritual growth, and notetaking will help you succeed.

Where to Take Notes

It is appropriate to take notes on God's Word at every opportunity. However, even this small discipline requires a little planning. Taking notes on scraps of paper, bulletin inserts, and offering envelopes will not result in the kind of growth which you are seeking. For this reason, a sample *Spiritual Journal* with a helpful notetaking section has been included in the appendix of this book.

The use of this *Journal* will help keep you from the experience of my good friend, a West Texas cattleman, who was at a Bible conference in Houston. A wonderful British Bible teacher was exhorting us from the Scriptures. As we walked across the street together, I asked my friend, "How is God speaking to you through this conference?" This man, who was in his seventies and wore a Stetson hat, cowboy boots, and a western suit, said, "Son, my cup is full and running over." That was his explanation of how greatly he was being blessed. About six weeks later, I ran into him in another city. When I asked, "How is your cup?" he pensively replied, "Had a hole in it."

Maybe you can identify with this experience. You went to a conference or attended a church service or a crusade and you were greatly blessed, only to discover a few days later that you felt empty again. Remember, your problem may not be a lack of dedication, but simply a lack of retention.

Why Take Notes?

Some people live the first year of their Christian lives over many times. Instead of growing, they end up on a treadmill, learning and forgetting the same lessons year after year. The object of spiritual growth is not to live the first year nine times, but to live nine progressive years of the Christian life!

According to a national survey, the average minister spends twenty hours per week in sermon preparation. When he realizes that Sunday after Sunday, his average church member will retain only three minutes of content from a thirty-minute sermon, it has to be discouraging. If you want to encourage your pastor, let him know that you are serious about listening. When you meet him at the door instead of saying, "I enjoyed the service," mention one specific verse, insight, or illustration that helped you. Tell him how God used the sermon to positively affect your life. Through this, he will know that you heard what the Holy Spirit was saying through the message.

Practical application is retention's best friend. When your actions and attitudes are positively affected, your recall will increase as well. Science has demonstrated that you remember 90 percent of what you *hear, read,* and then *do.* Your spiritual objective should therefore focus on James 1:22 (J. B. Phillips), which says, "Don't only hear the message, but put it into practice; otherwise you are merely deluding yourselves." Your first practical step toward victory is simply beginning a lifestyle of taking good notes.

The objective of notetaking is not to outline the sermon or the Sunday school lesson. What matters is recording what the Holy Spirit is teaching you personally as you listen to the Word of God. Write down the things that will make a difference in your life—insights you can actually apply. The test of good listening and good application is life itself. When you leave church or a Bible study, you need to go out better prepared to live positively and effectively.

Reverence for Scripture

Spiritual growth occurs when we meditate upon what God says and then apply it in our daily lives. Because this is true we need to cultivate an attitude like the people of Ezra's day. They hungered for a word from God! Nehemiah 8 says: "And Ezra, the Priest, brought the Law before the congregation, and he read therein from morning until mid-day, and the ears of the people were attentive. And when he read, all the people stood up, and Ezra blessed the Lord, the great God, and all the people answered, 'Amen, Amen'." [5]

Why did they stand up? Wouldn't they have been more comfortable sitting down? Yes. But they stood up out of respect for God's Word. Can you imagine such a congregation? Can you believe that they chose to stand up all that time? Today it is sometimes hard to get people to come to listen, even in air-conditioned comfort, but to Ezra's congregation, inconvenience didn't matter.

"When Ezra read, all the people stood up. . . ." These words took on a fresh meaning for me several years ago. Each part of the world has its own unique customs, and I was once in an African congregation with a very unusual tradition. No one had prepared me for the fact that out of reverence for God's Word the congregation would automatically stand every time the Bible was read. That day I covered numerous verses while preaching. You can imagine my surprise when—everyone was standing and sitting, standing and sitting! I had no idea what was happening. Later, the interpreter explained their tradition to me. Time did not allow me to become comfortable with the custom, but the respect that congregation held for the Bible convinced me that too many of us do not value the sacredness of God's Word.

In recent years some countries have been blessed with an amazing array of up-to-date translations which include a wide assortment of chain references, concordances, and other helpful information. With all these modern blessings, you must carefully guard against taking your Bible for granted. The privilege of reading its sacred pages is still beyond the reach of a large percentage of the world's population. Only in the light of this overwhelming truth can we begin to appreciate the value of its availability.

The scarcity of Bibles in other countries was vividly brought to my attention several years ago as counselors were being trained for an evangelistic campaign in a West African country. Although Christians had been in the area for decades, the nation was largely made up of animists.[6] Being unfamiliar with many of their country's unique problems, I wrote ahead to organize the crusade in a routine manner. Our standard Bible study requirements caused the counselors in training to walk for miles, sometimes barefooted, to join a friend who owned a prized possession—a Bible. Months later, when I arrived to preach, my heart was deeply moved when I realized how insensitive we had been due to our Western assumption that every Christian had a Bible. These dear brothers and sisters would have to work a week or more to afford a copy of the Scriptures.

In Ezra's day, the problem was even more pronounced. People had to gather to listen to God's Word from the handwritten scrolls which had been painstakingly copied.

Carrying Your Bible

Owning a Bible is a privilege, and carrying it with you is a witness in itself. Spurgeon, a famous British Christian, used to say, "Carry your Bible with you every place you go, because it will preach a thousand sermons a day!" How true this is. When people see your Bible, they automatically think of its message; and the Holy Spirit will apply conviction, comfort, or hope to their hearts.

As a student, I learned this valuable lesson. One day in class, my Bible toppled off my other books and landed on the floor. My agnostic teacher immediately stopped the class, saying, "Billie, your Bible has fallen on the floor." Though she had never received Christ as her Savior, her deep respect for what He stood for caused her to spontaneously honor His words of truth. This simple occurrence provided a natural opportunity for me to talk with her privately. I explained that if the Bible were already meaningful to her, its inspired message would affect her even more when she came to know its Author. Though she was much older and also my teacher, it was obvious from the look in her eyes that she received that suggestion with genuine appreciation.

A Godly Attitude

You will increase your joy in reading the Bible and hearing its message preached and taught if you learn an important secret.

In Memphis, Tennessee, I have a friend who was invited to be a guest speaker in a church which is known for its long services. After an hour of congregational singing and testimonies, a beautiful piano solo was played. A lady stood up in the back of the congregation and reverently said, "Yes, Lord, yes." Time passed, and another person stood and said the same thing. After several minutes, a large percentage of the congregation had stood to their feet and said, "Yes, Lord, yes."

My friend was perplexed because he had not heard a question. Finally his host, a well-known black pastor, looked heavenward and said, "Father, we have given You our response in advance. Now speak to us through Your messenger and tell us what it is You desire for us to do." The secret to joy in worship is listening with a prepared heart. What God is looking for in every Christian's attitude is faith expressed in a *pre-determined will to obey.*

Have you ever attended church when the last thing you felt like doing was worshiping the Lord? We need to guard our frame of mind and worship with a spirit of expectancy. This requires planning ahead, because invariably the whole world seems to clamor for our attention immediately prior to worship. What a difference it will make in your life when you come to church saying, "Yes, Lord, yes." When this is the attitude of your heart, God will begin to use your life in wonderful new ways!

Too many of us listen to God's Word as if we were partaking of a smorgasbord. We want to select a little bit of this and a little bit of that from the Bible, but we do not come with a pre-determined will to receive whatever God says we need and then apply it in our lives. All too often, our attitude is something like this: "Lord, I want to hear what You have to say to me as long as it fits what I already plan to do." The net result is that we ask Him to bless what we want to be blessed. We try to ignore what we do not want to hear. Mature worship is putting ourselves under the authority of Jesus Christ by saying, "Yes, Lord, yes. I'm available; I'm willing; I'm eager to do what You want me to do."

Having believed in Christ and having received Him as your Savior, your love for Him will be evidenced by listening to His Word and walking in obedience to His will. Because He came to give you an abundant life, His leadership will always direct you to the highest plain of fulfillment. We have His unfailing promise: "I will instruct you and teach you in the way which you should go; I will counsel you with My eye upon you." [7]

Using the format of the *Spiritual Journal* found on pages 101 through 132, will you commit yourself to the Lord to grow in your faith by taking notes on what you hear from the Bible during the next four weeks?

____Yes

____No

"Faith comes from what is preached, and what is preached comes from the word of Christ."

Romans 10:17, JB

3
The Perfect Example

Very early in the morning, while it was still dark, Jesus got up, left the house and went off to a solitary place, where he prayed. (Mark 1:35, NIV)

The Lord's perfect life is an example for all mankind to follow. The world has had many teachers, but only one Christ—His actions were as inspired as the words which He spoke.

The Example of Jesus

He started His day with the Father, not only because He wanted to, but because in His humanity He actually needed to. Each time He departed for a season alone in prayer and personal fellowship with the Father, His human needs were met. Beyond that, He was showing His disciples how to live victoriously. He arose early on this particular morning (Mark 1:35) and chose to be totally alone. On the day before, He had preached in Capernaum, freed a man possessed by demons, healed Peter's mother-in-law, and preached again to a huge crowd where great numbers of spiritually, physically, and emotionally sick people were healed.[1] It is an understatement to say that His schedule had been busy.

Everyone wanted to be with Him—the sick and disturbed, new followers, disciples in training, and hangers-on; they were all pressing in upon Him. To get any time alone with the Father, Jesus literally had to get up while it was still dark and slip away while the others were sleeping.

This devotional practice was essential in the Lord's earthly life, because He lived in total dependence upon the spiritual strength given to Him by His Father. He carefully reminded His disciples that no work He did was of Himself and that no word He ever spoke was His own. He credited the Father with everything accomplished in His ministry.[2] He literally lived each moment in total dependence upon His Father. Ironically, our Savior who spoke only of dependence was seen by the Jewish leaders of the day as the most independent man they had ever met! [3]

During the Lord's solitary times of prayer He was sometimes interrupted. Such was the case on this particular morning. "And Simon and his companions hunted for Him; and they found Him, and said to Him, 'Everyone is looking for You'." [4] Several important lessons can be seen in this experience, but first concentrate on the person of Christ.

What really happened when He was interrupted? Visualize the Lord talking to His Father. Consider the fact that He was filled with the Holy Spirit without measure.[5] Allow the exalted meaning of this verse to permeate your mind. "For in Him (Christ) all the fulness of Deity dwells in bodily form." [6] Everything that God is was present in the life of Christ. Since prayer is a conversation, one could accurately say that Peter and the other apostles *unknowingly* interrupted a holy time of communion shared by God the Father, God the Son, and God the Holy Spirit. To be sure, this was a most holy moment.

When the Lord's prayer time was interrupted, He demonstrated what our reaction should be. He did not chide those who intruded upon His time with the Father. He did not allow the interruption to upset His spirit or ruin His day. He did not quit seeking times alone with His Father. His lifestyle remained consistent yet flexible, regardless of the outward circumstances, but how does this relate to us as Christians today?

Practical Devotions

The Lord Jesus and the early Christians lived in that pre-electric era when people normally went to bed early and got up early. If they wanted to do anything at night they had to build a fire or use a small oil-burning lantern. Although Jesus rose early, it was probably after getting a good night's rest. The point of this passage is not to rise before the sun comes up, but rather to start your day with God whenever your day normally begins. This principle will hold true for shift workers, night watchmen, and people of every vocation.

No specific hour is established in the Bible for your daily Quiet Time. You do not have to be like the famous British cricketer, C. T. Studd, who is said to have read the Bible by candlelight in the early morning hours. I will never forget what a guilt trip I went on once after hearing a marvelous sermon on the Quiet Time. After that service, I thought the only way to be spiritual was to get up at 4:00 A.M. and read the Bible by candlelight! The key to spiritual growth is not how *early* but how expectantly and consistently one meets with the Father.

Medical science has discovered that all of us have a biological clock. Our bodies actually require differing amounts of sleep in order to work at peak efficiency. I have a good friend from Africa who only needs four or five hours of sleep per night, but most people need seven or eight.

Alexander the Great had a very unusual biological clock. It is said that when needed, he could sleep 72 hours and work 72 hours. This was one of the ways he won his battles. He wore out one army after another! No one else could concentrate on the fight that long. He learned to use his strengths and limitations, and when he died at the age of 32 he had already accomplished a great deal.

It is important to get to know about your own sleep requirements, so you can plan ahead to be wide awake for your Quiet Times. Eventually in your Christian experience, no matter how dedicated you are, you will face the reality of fatigue. The Lord faced it. One afternoon He went to sleep in a boat [7] and demonstrated to His disciples that when exhausted, the most spiritual thing you can do is rest!

Relating this principle to your own Quiet Time, remember that trying to keep one eye open while reading the Bible is like attempting to talk to someone when you are only half awake. Under normal circumstances, if a person really loves you and sees that you are exhausted, he will want you to go ahead and sleep. God's attitude is clearly revealed in the Scripture which says He "gives His beloved sleep." [8]

Getting Started

Let me challenge you to join the countless millions whose lives have been changed by beginning their day with a Quiet Time. Ten to fifteen minutes each morning will make an amazing difference in your day. Why not stop right now and dedicate "these special minutes" to God. Give Him the beginnings of all your future days. Ask Him to continually remind you of the important commitment you are making. As you pray, thank Him for the high privilege of consciously spending time in His presence.

All spiritual growth is based upon *decisions.* The choice you are making to begin a daily Quiet Time is one you will never regret. Through it, you will grow in fellowship with God and in your ability to minister to your fellow man.

Every journey starts with a first step, and a Quiet Time begins by simply waking up and getting out of bed in the morning! I am reminded of the story about a man who always stayed in bed while trying to read the Bible. One day he confessed that "something came up," and he missed his Quiet Time. His confession was supposedly overheard by his guardian angel, who candidly remarked, "Something came up, indeed! It was big and white, and it looked exactly like a sheet!"

The opposite side of fatigue is oversleeping. Some people are "spendaholics." They spend God's money on this, that, and the other, and then they have nothing left to give. Others are "workaholics." They work, work, work, until no time is left to be with God because they have substituted activity for worship.

Then there is the "sleepaholic," who misses his time with God because he is a glutton for sleep. If you are a sleepaholic, let me suggest that you memorize Proverbs 6:9, which says, "How long will you lie down, O sluggard? When will you arise from your sleep?" When you commit that verse to memory, the Holy Spirit will use it time after time to awaken you when you are rolling from one side of your bed to the other in the morning. I can assure you this is true, because He has used this verse with me on more than one occasion.

"I overslept" is perhaps the most commonly used excuse for not having a Quiet Time. Over the years, as I have taught on this subject, approximately 15 percent of the conferees have said that they are very sluggish in the mornings, 15 percent have said they wake up bright and eager to begin the day. Another 70 percent say they get up reasonably well but they still have trouble being alert. A Quiet Time is intended to be fun, so let me give you a few practical suggestions on this matter of being awake and alert. While some of these suggestions are more serious than others, all of them can be helpful.

Analyze what gets you awake in the morning. For my wife, Ruth, it is coffee. She frequently drinks it before or during her Quiet Time. For men, let me recommend Mennen Skin Bracer. Don't drink it—just splash it on your face, neck, elbows, and kneecaps, and you will feel like running around the room. It's tremendous! For the same effect, ladies can use Charles of the Ritz Tingling Astringent.

Exercise is also good. Recently in Korea, a veteran missionary showed me his tried and proven method. He shakes his hands vigorously while running in place for one thousand steps. This is followed by an ice cold shower! In favorable climates, a brisk morning walk before Bible reading will accomplish the same objective. The Bible says, "discipline yourself for the purpose of godliness," [9] so whatever approach you use, make up your mind in advance to carry it through.

For those who have a particular aversion to mid-winter devotions, I have heard of one unique wake-up approach. If you sleep on the right-hand side of the bed, put your right leg out from under the cover first. If you do not get up immediately, just let it hang off the edge of the bed, and it will grow uncomfortable after a while. Soon you will swing your left leg over to join it. Before you know it, you will be up washing your face and getting ready for the day.

Remember this thought: even though the Scripture says, "Be still, and know that I am God," [10] let me suggest that you not be *too* still. The objective is to get out of bed to read and pray. If you do not, your quiet time will inevitably be too quiet!

Evening Devotions

There are several hazards in having your devotions at night. I am not saying that God will not bless it, but it often amounts to giving Him the "leftovers" of your day. You are already tired. You have given your best to the world, your job, and the people around you. But the One who deserves the most receives the least. Make note of four hazards related to having your devotions at night: energy spent, pillow soft, lights dim, print small! I have experienced every one of these hazards and have unintentionally fallen off to sleep.

As a young Christian, I attempted to have my Quiet Time at night simply because I didn't know any better. Like so many people, I would sleep until the last minute and rush to class in the mornings. For years, my only Scripture reading and prayer was at night. My grandmother had given me a large Bible. One evening as I was reading it the pillow seemed so soft and the light looked so dim that I soon fell asleep with the Bible on my chest. I didn't move until the next morning. The big Bible was still on my chest, and in the zone between sleep and wakefulness I kept subconsciously thinking, "Something is wrong!" The Bible's weight produced a strange feeling. I remember opening my eyes very slowly, and seeing the words "Holy Bible" upside down. A sentimental feeling swept over me: "I slept all night with a Bible on my chest!" There's one thing you can be sure of—that's not the way to increase your spirituality!

Charlie Riggs of the Billy Graham team has said, "The Word of God has to get into your mind, and then make an 18-inch trip down into your heart." How true that is. You have to be alert enough to think through what you are reading if it is going to affect the way you live.

When I heard about the value of having a Quiet Time, I accepted a six-weeks' challenge to begin spending ten minutes each morning with God. It was like eating honey—once you taste it, you want more. The Psalmist said, "How sweet are Thy words to my taste! Yes, sweeter than honey to my mouth!" [11] As time passed, I came to understand the testimony of Jeremiah: ". . . Thy words became for me a joy and the delight of my heart . . ." [12]

You can *begin* your day with God and *end* it with Him as well. If you want to read and pray at night, that's great, as long as it is not your only Quiet Time. Enjoy your spiritual cake in the morning and the icing before you go to sleep at night!

If, while reading this chapter, you have consecrated the beginning of your days to God, you will find that making a specific commitment for the next four weeks will solidify that important decision. For this reason, I want you to prayerfully *date* today's commitment:

Unless providentially hindered, I will begin each morning, starting tomorrow, with not less than 10 to 15 minutes alone with God.

_____

Date

To follow through with this life-changing decision, you will need to read the brief additional instructions and use the daily Quiet Time forms found in the sample *Spiritual Journal* section in the appendix of this book, pages 101–132. May God prepare your heart for the high calling of time with Him. Remember, "God is utterly dependable and it is he who has called you into fellowship with His Son Jesus Christ, our Lord." [13]

4
The Secret of Godliness

Discipline yourself for the purpose of godliness. (*1 Timothy 4:7b*)

No one reaches godliness by accident. It is only as you seek personal purity, determine to be holy, and allow Christ to be in control that the victorious Christian life becomes *experientially* yours. Spiritual growth, unlike physical growth, is the product of personal commitment. We decide to discipline ourselves for "the purpose of godliness." [1] As we make Christ-honoring decisions, He gives us all the power we need to live them out.

This new life is one which the secular world cannot fully understand.[2] Paul describes its uniqueness in 2 Corinthians 5:17, "Therefore if any man be in Christ, he is a new creature: old things are passed away; behold, all things are become new." [3] Paul's personal testimony reflects His complete change in values. "Whatever things were gain to me, those things I have counted as loss . . ." But why? ". . . in view of the surpassing value of knowing Christ Jesus my Lord . . ." [4] Christians have a new and different mindset. The Scripture says, "If you have been raised up with Christ, . . . Set your mind on the things above, not on the things that are on earth." [5]

The new thoughts, actions, and deep affections that come with receiving Christ are nurtured by our close fellowship with Him. Like most new disciples, the first verse I ever learned was John 3:16.[6] Years later, a friend showed me 1 Corinthians 1:9 and explained its wonderful meaning. It became my second memory verse: "God is utterly dependable, and it is he who has called you into fellowship with His Son Jesus Christ, our Lord." [7] It was through this passage that I discovered that every Christian has a calling—yes, the high calling of fellowship with Christ.

God Desires Our Fellowship

Why set aside Quiet Times for prayer and daily Bible reading? Because God Himself is faithfully calling us into a life of fellowship with His Son. To disappoint that holy desire on the part of God for even one day would be a tragedy. In John 4:23 His desire for fellowship is emphasized, this time by Jesus, who said, "An hour is coming . . . when the true worshipers shall worship the Father in spirit and truth; for such people the Father seeks to be His worshipers." Fellowship, our highest calling, is at the very heart of our worship and everything else we do as God's children. Through it we are participants in His highest purpose for life.

The daily Quiet Time is not a program designed by men, nor is it a legalistic ritual based on tradition. It is the outward response of our innate desire to truly know God. Listen to the words of the Apostle Paul after having been a Christian for many years. The hunger of his heart was to deepen that fellowship: "That I may know him, and the power of his resurrection, and the fellowship of his sufferings. . . ." [8] Paul wanted to know every aspect of having a close relationship with his Creator.

Love is like that. Married couples will quickly testify that after having known and loved each other for years they are still learning to appreciate new aspects of one another's personalities. Love is spelled T-I-M-E. To really know someone requires years of fellowship in a wide variety of circumstances. This same rule applies to your walk with God.

The Reassurance of His Love

Hunger for God is as old as man himself, but few have expressed this longing with the clarity of Moses. In his beautiful prayer psalm he says, "O satisfy us in the morning with thy steadfast love that we may rejoice and be glad all of our days." [9] He grasped an essential truth about God's love: It is steadfast, unchanging, and secure.

Morning by morning Moses had experienced the secret of *joy* and *gladness.* He was walking in close fellowship with the God he loved in spite of all the difficulties the world could hurl in his direction. Put yourself in his place: at the age of 80, he was responsible for moving 600,000 men and their families [10] to the country of Canaan. The hostile Egyptian army was behind him, a burning desert lay in front of him, and he had very little food and water. Humanly speaking, he had nothing but problems. In addition to all these obstacles, the people were also unhappy most of the time. He bore the heaviest kind of responsibility in the worst kind of working environment. It was in this setting that he learned the supreme value of spending his mornings with God.

Wouldn't you like to be inwardly satisfied at the dawning of each new day? Think about a delicious meal that satisfies your hunger or a drink that satisfies your thirst. The daily Quiet Time is designed to satisfy your hunger for God Himself. If you have responsibilities, live in a challenging environment, or need to be reminded that God loves you, the same joy that Moses experienced is there for the taking. You and I are God's children, too!

If Christians cannot live as proof of an abundant, positive joy, who in this world can? The person in your mirror has the right to be happy! You have been redeemed and are now God's child. You are free to live out your potential to the fullest extent. Ephesians 2:10 says, "For we are His workmanship, created in Christ Jesus for good works, which God prepared beforehand, that we should walk in them." You are a special person with a special mission. Each and every morning, God wants to remind you of who you are in Christ.

Our Need for Direction

Psalm 143:8 is one of many practical verses in the Bible. It deals specifically with having a daily Quiet Time. David says, "Cause me to hear thy lovingkindness in the morning; for in thee do I trust: cause me to know the way wherein I should walk; for I lift up my soul unto thee." [11] If there was ever a man in the Bible who needed to have a daily Quiet Time for guidance, it was David. When he says, "I lift up my soul unto thee," it literally means, "I place my life in Your hands."

Consider David, a man whose life was lived in constant conflict—a man's man, fearless and decisive. Why did he pray for direction and help? Because he grasped the reality of his own need.

As a shepherd boy, David learned to trust God when protecting his flock from dangerous animals. While still a teenager, he faced the giant soldier, Goliath, with only a sling. As a young man, he spent years running from King Saul, who had once been his friend. He lived in danger from the Philistines throughout adulthood. And in later life, two of his own children (Absalom and Adonijah) sought to take his throne by violence. Though he lived in crisis, David became a man after God's own heart,[12] a man God deeply loved. Even when he sank to the very depths of sin,[13] he rebounded and received the forgiveness for which he longed. He prayed daily for practical direction, for he had tasted failure and he was well aware of his need.

Perhaps the best wisdom is learning from the mistakes of others and not making them yourself. Failing that, at least we can learn from our own poor choices and not repeat the same sin over and over again. Someone said that we Christians all learn to pray eventually: the question is whether we will be praying for *guidance* or *forgiveness.* To re-state an old maxim, an ounce of guidance is worth more than a pound of forgiveness.

As a new Christian, I learned this lesson in the school of hard knocks. It seemed that every night my prayers would begin the same way: "Lord, forgive me for all my sins." Unfortunately, my list never included my failure to seek His guidance. The sin of presumptuousness is subtle but real, and it leaves millions of Christians living in mediocrity. God wants us to go into the day with the benefit of His counsel, but all too often we end our day in needless defeat, simply because we have neglected to seek His direction. God's guidance is as generously available as His forgiveness. He says, "I will instruct you and teach you in the way which you should go; I will counsel you with My eye upon you." [14]

Dry Spells

No matter how much you love the Lord or the depth of your dedication, there will be times of spiritual dryness in your life. Usually these will merely be the result of physical fatigue. On other occasions, they may be the result of boredom, unresolved conflicts, medical difficulties, or unconfessed sin. David suffered acutely from middle-aged boredom, and Moses chafed under the unending ingratitude of those to whom he ministered. No one is exempt from times of spiritual dryness. Though these periods are not desirable, God can use them to teach you valuable lessons. It is often as the result of these occasions that you can most clearly see His faithfulness.

How can dry times be avoided? Consistency is the key! A good athlete does not work out only when he feels like it. He trains daily because he knows that exercise is in his best interest and will make the difference in winning or losing to his competition. The same is true with farming or any other worthwhile activity. The Bible says, ". . . let us not get tired of doing what is right, for after a while we will reap a harvest of blessing if we don't get discouraged and give up." [15]

Let's assume that you make a spiritual commitment to keep growing, but you miss your Quiet Time for some good reason. The devil will try to turn that perfectly legitimate situation into the beginning of a dry spell. His tactics will probably operate something like this: he'll say, "If you really were a dedicated Christian, you would have gotten up this morning and had your Quiet Time. You made a commitment to spend time with God, and this morning you didn't do it." He will carefully avoid the fact that you stayed up late the night before doing something important which was spiritually on target. If you are in the will of God staying up late, you can also be in the will of God sleeping late! You need to memorize this verse: "There is therefore now no condemnation for those who are in Christ Jesus." [16] Satan does not have the right to condemn you as a Christian because you do not belong to him. You are God's child.

"Spiritual Spankings"

Have you ever given your neighbor's child a spanking? It is a hazardous venture, because only your most discerning friends will appreciate and affirm your helping them with discipline. Many people would be offended by it. By and large, we spank our own children because they are our responsibility. In the same way, the Bible says, "God chastises those whom He loves." [17] God gives us our spiritual spankings because we are His and He loves us. Satan has no right to administer correction, condemnation, or anything else to you as a Christian; so be careful not to let him discourage you as you walk with Christ.

A seminary professor once shared a principle which has been extremely helpful to me over the years. He taught me that "God convicts in specifics . . . and Satan condemns in generalities." For example, if you missed several Quiet Times for poor reasons, Satan might say, "Jim, you just don't have what it takes to be dedicated. To be honest, I don't think you are going to make it. If you really loved God, you'd do better." Satan will try to condemn you and make you feel defeated. Count on it. It's predictable!

In contrast, the Holy Spirit might say something like this, "Jim, you are My child and I love you, but you missed a real blessing this morning. I had something special to share with you from My Word. Be careful not to keep missing these times together, because you will not receive a blessing if you're not there."

God will always call attention to your omission, and He will also convict you about the need to correct the problem, but He will never *condemn* you for committing the sin. Satan will condemn you as a person because he wants to erode your self-worth. In contrast, God will *convict* you about the sinfulness of an act but at the same time, He will continually affirm you as a person and build your self-worth.

Failing to understand this basic difference has caused many people to get the activities of God and Satan mixed up. God operates out of concern, with man's best interest at heart, but Satan plays by a different set of game rules. His desire is to weaken your witness and to entice you into an undisciplined lifestyle of spiritual compromise. He uses condemnation as a tool to achieve his purpose. He wants you to be negative about yourself, your friends, the church, the Bible, and if possible—even about life itself. His objective is to get you discouraged, so you will quit trying to grow.

Be smart, and remember that the enemy has no power over you whatsoever unless you give it to him of your own free will. "There is no condemnation to those who are in Christ Jesus." We fight a *defeated* enemy, and "We are more than conquerors through Him who loved us." [18]

The secret of achieving godliness can be found in a lifestyle of spiritual *consistency*. The matchless life which has been made possible through Christ's death and suffering is already ours potentially, and it becomes ours *experientially* as we choose it on a day-to-day basis. What kind of life do you really want? This is the issue. Everything required for your happiness has already been provided. You are free as God's child to live a life of incomparable victory! The Scriptures declare, "I press toward the goal for the mark of the high calling of God in Christ Jesus." [19]

5
Principles for Living in Victory

But in all these things we overwhelmingly conquer through Him who loved us. (Romans 8:37)

PRINCIPLE #1: *Growth Comes Slowly*

"And let endurance have its perfect result, that you may be perfect and complete, lacking in nothing." [1]

As newlyweds, Ruth and I had the unique experience of being houseguests of the Billy Grahams on Christmas Day. My spiritual dad, Grady Wilson, and Billy Graham, his lifelong friend, decided to play golf that afternoon. In order not to reveal my poor golf game, I quickly volunteered to be Dr. Graham's caddy. He had recently had surgery and seemed pleased with the suggestion. As we covered the mountainous North Carolina course, I took every opportunity to ask questions. Once when he sliced the ball, I said something like, "Life is sometimes like that, isn't it?" to which he replied, "Yes, some go off to the left, and others to the right." He described how those who move to either extreme diminish their own capacity for letting God use them.

As we walked, I asked him if there were still many verses in the Bible that gave him trouble. He said there were some which he had been praying to understand for over twenty-five years. He went on to express the amazing truth—that when you really need to understand a passage, "God opens it up and it blossoms like a beautiful flower. In His own time, He reveals the hidden meaning and beauty of each facet of His Word."

Jesus illustrated this truth in His model prayer.[2] He taught us to pray in an attitude of patience. He didn't say, "Give us this day our *full week's* bread in advance." We were told to trust Him for one day at a time. Spiritually speaking, *daily* bread is God's only means of provision. When the Lord called Himself the "bread of life," [3] He sought to deepen our understanding of the reality that our daily bread is spiritual as well as physical. He said, "Man does not live on bread alone, but on every word that comes from the mouth of God." [4]

For most of us, eating is enjoyable. On the average, we eat about a thousand meals each year. The physical changes produced by eating take place so slowly that from one day to the next they cannot be seen. But our bodies are never static. Each day we change.

Remember the impatience of childhood? Next year seemed an eternity away. Only as we mature do we come to understand that both spiritual and physical growth come slowly.

PRINCIPLE #2: *Use Common Sense*

Old-fashioned common sense is a virtue which will help ensure a life of spiritual victory. For fun, imagine I am walking down a street in your town and you see tears streaming down my cheeks. Concerned, you ask, "Billie, why are you crying? You look so sad!" Forlornly I reply, "I missed lunch!" Then you ask, "What's the big deal about missing lunch?" I say, "I made a commitment years ago to be an eater. I promised to be consistent! But today I blew it; I missed lunch. I just don't have what it takes. I'm through; I'll never eat again."

If you miss a meal, you simply compensate for it later. You do not stop eating. If you miss your daily Quiet Time, the same principle applies. Simply have a longer prayer time and more

Bible reading later. This could be that night or even the next morning.

There is nothing legalistic about eating your favorite meal. Why? Because eating is a pleasure. Just as your physical hunger reminds you to visit the refrigerator, your spiritual hunger reminds you to read the Bible. Self-imposed starvation and malnutrition are as foolish spiritually as they are physically, so use common sense and feed yourself.

PRINCIPLE #3: *Guard Your Affections*

Some time ago I was talking with a fellow minister about the importance of Christ being in first place in our lives. Matthew 6:33 says, "Seek ye first the kingdom of God . . ." [5] I asked, "What do you think this verse really means?" I will never forget his answer. He said, "Billie, Christ doesn't mean first place in a traditional sense. What if you went home to your wife and said, 'Ruth, I want you to know how much I love you. You are in first place in my life. However, I want you to know about Mary Lou, Jane, Rose, and Jeanette. They are in second, third, fourth, and fifth place!' " I got the point. Do you think Ruth would be happy just being in first place? Not at all. A wife or a husband wants to be your only sweetheart, not just the first one on the list.

This is the spirit of Matthew 6:33. Christ wants to be first, and He wants to be all. His call to discipleship is always clear and always has been. He said, "Unless you love Me more than your father, your mother, your wife, and your own life also, you cannot be My disciple." [6] This was not a new teaching but an echo of the first commandment, "Love the Lord your God with all your heart and with all your soul and with all your mind." [7] As we learn to love God with all that we are, He can begin to love others through us. Because He lives in us, there is an inexhaustible supply of love available for us to share with those close to us and those around the world. In His parting challenge in the Upper Room, He reminded His disciples of His new commandment: ". . . love one another, even as I have loved you . . ." [8]

Spiritual victory is achieved by allowing God to re-order our priorities and affections. In Colossians 3:2, Paul instructed us with these words, "Set your mind on the things above, not on the things that are on earth." If you want to find out if Christ is in first place, examine three areas of your life—your thoughts, your time, and your giving.

Your Thoughts

What do you enjoy thinking about? In Philippians 2:5, you are challenged to "Let this mind be in you, which was also in Christ Jesus." [9] The text goes on to say that the Lord humbled Himself to become a servant. Do you enjoy thinking of new ways to serve Him? In Philippians 4:8, the Bible says, "Finally, brethren, whatever is true, whatever is honorable, whatever is right, whatever is pure, whatever is lovely, whatever is of good repute, if there is any excellence and if anything worthy of praise, let your mind dwell on these things." Your mind is a mirror of your affections. When you truly seek His kingdom, you will know it. Your own thoughts will reveal it.

The Scriptures teach us this important principle: As a man "thinks in his heart, so is he." [10] We become like the things we think about. For this reason, the Bible says, "Keep your heart with all diligence; for out of it are the issues of life." [11] You may be asking, "How do I keep my heart with diligence?" When the Bible refers to the heart, it is usually a reference to that part of your mind where life's deepest decisions are made. This is also the place where your affections are formed. In a spiritual sense, you are protecting your heart when you guard your mind. It is a matter of both mental and spiritual hygiene.

The Scripture warns, "If any man love the world, the love of the Father is not in him." [12] This teaching is easy to understand in light of the First Commandment, "Love the Lord your God with all your heart." [13] As a person gives his love to God, he has less left for the sinful things in the world around him.

Your Time

Do you enjoy being with God in times of fellowship, recreation, worship, and training? The first Christians completely reordered their lives. They left everything they had to spend every possible hour with the Master. In those periods together He taught them how to be "fishers of men." Mark 3:14a says, "And He appointed twelve, that they might be *with Him. . . .*" Their great service to the world followed their time spent in His presence.

Though the radical nature of the apostles' calling in most cases will not resemble the specific way God deals with you, the spirit of your calling is the same as Peter's, James', and John's. To them, their time with Christ was so valuable that they literally climbed mountains and walked the long, winding, dusty roads of Judah and Galilee to be near Him.[14]

It is sobering to think that some Christians, who look forward to heaven, will not rise fifteen minutes early or attend services on Sunday to be with Him here on earth. I have often wondered what it is they expect in heaven that makes them want to go there. If they do not cherish the music of praise and the fellowship of His children, or love to hear the eternal truths of His Word, how strange the surroundings of heaven will seem.

The Apostle John, describing that future time, says, "And I heard, as it were, the voice of a great multitude . . . as the sound of mighty peals of thunder, saying, 'Hallelujah! For the Lord our God, the Almighty, reigns'." [15] Every moment spent praising Him and getting to know Him at the deepest human level is time that will have eternal value, because your relationship with Him will last forever. If you find yourself too busy for that kind of fellowship, you are too busy!

Your Giving

"Where your treasure is, there will your heart be also." [16] If you want to know what is important to you, look at your checkbook stubs. Most of us are afraid to do that, because we do not want to face the truth. They would show that our highest motivation and true goal for making money is not really the Great Commission. Our affections are still earthbound. We may suspect this and sometimes even grow a little concerned about it, but God cannot use us mightily, nor trust us as He would like to, until the "Goliath of ownership" has been slain in our lives.

As your daily Quiet Time becomes consistent and you begin to understand the principles on which God operates, you will discover that giving is at the very heart of His nature. Your personal spiritual growth can be measured by the answer to this question: "How much am I becoming like Him?" As you are conformed to His image, your new attitude will resemble that of David's day: ". . . the people rejoiced because they had offered so willingly, for they made their offering to the Lord with a whole heart. . . ." [17]

Soon this will dawn on you: every moment of your life, every possession you value, every friendship you hold dear, every accomplishment you have achieved, have come to you only through God's love. When this dawning occurs, you will be overwhelmed! You will be gripped with the desire to give back to Him in return. Did He not give you the mind, the will, and the strength to make everything you do and have possible?

The psalmist says, "The earth is the Lord's, and all it contains, the world, and those who dwell in it." [18] Christ owns the 100 percent; yet He generously gives us 90 percent to invest, enjoy, and live on. The tithe, 10 percent of our income, is all that He requires, but a Christian's most joyful giving is often done well beyond that minimum. Why? Because of the knowledge that these funds will be used to help fulfill the Great Commission and bring the Good News of Jesus Christ to every nation of the world.[19]

In chapter 29 of First Chronicles, you will discover a fact which has always struck me as humorous, even though David expressed these thoughts in sincere worship and praise. In verse 12 he says, "Both riches and honor come from Thee . . ." and then, "who am I and who are my people that we should be able to offer as generously as this? For all things come from Thee, and from Thy hand we have given Thee" (verse 14).

The only thing we have to give God is what He has already given us. This is why we can never overgive or outgive God. One of my close friends says, "When we give to God, He is also giving to us. He just uses a bigger shovel!"

One Father's Day I had an experience which brought this message home. My ten-year-old, Heather, decided to go shopping. For two years she had saved the money we had given her for making good grades. When I walked through the door there were house slippers, pajamas, a robe, a new shirt, a tie (not a tie I would have picked, but a modern tie she thought I needed), and a shaving kit. The shaving kit contained soap, perfume, shaving lotion, and just about everything you could want. She was standing there beaming with delight! I picked her up, hugged her, and thanked her from the bottom of my heart. Then I asked, "Honey, how much did you spend?" (a typical father's question). The reply was, "Everything I had." I thought to myself, *How impractically wonderful!*

Love is like that. Do you think I would ever knowingly let Heather go broke or suffer for having given me everything she had? Obviously as her father I have the power to give her back what she gave me many times over. What thrills me is the fact that she did the giving on her own, and that she did all she could. That I will never forget.

So the deepest truth about giving is that both the 10 percent and the 90 percent are actually His. Everything you are is His. When your unrighteousness was exchanged for His goodness,[20] the title deed of your life was passed to God forever.[21] Your physical body became His earthly temple. You were no longer your own, for you had been bought with a price.[22] From that point forward, you were treated as His very own child. When you try to shower Him with your love and your gifts, though they may seem large to you they are never more than a small fraction of what He has already given. Why does God rejoice in our giving? Not because He needs it, but because He wants to see us become like Him, and He—is a giver! "For God so loved the world that He gave . . ."[23]

PRINCIPLE #4: *Carve Islands in Your Day*

"But the news about Him was spreading even farther, and great multitudes were gathering to hear Him and to be healed of their sicknesses. But He Himself would often slip away to the wilderness and pray."[24] The news about Christ was spreading. His ministry was growing, and His responsibilities were increasing. When the pressures of life begin to build, we are presented with two options: We can either control our circumstances or we can allow them to control us. The Lord Jesus modeled the right decision.

Paradoxically, the more you have to do, the less time you have to do it in. Recently I had lunch with a famous Bible teacher who is much in demand in many parts of the world. He said, "Billie, I have a tremendous frustration in my life, because this year I have received 2,000 invitations to speak. It is hard for me to know which of them the Holy Spirit intends for me to accept." As the impact of his ministry has increased, his need for wisdom and guidance has increased in direct proportion.

We have already discussed the importance of beginning your day with God. However, the Lord not only started His day in prayer, but as one busy businessman has put it, He "carved islands in His day." At every opportunity, He would slip away to be with the Father.

Even on the most noted day of His public ministry, Jesus planned ahead to have an island of time alone. Having fed 5,000 men and their families with only five loaves and two fish, He spoke to the multitude ". . . teaching them many things." [25] It was late in the day when the disciples picked up twelve baskets of broken pieces of bread and fish. Immediately, the Scripture says, ". . . He made His disciples get into the boat and go ahead of Him to Bethsaida (the other side of the Sea of Galilee), while He Himself was sending the multitudes away. And after bidding them farewell, He departed to the mountain to pray." [26]

Jesus broke all precedent on this occasion. Normally, He would dismiss the multitude, then take the twelve to some quiet spot where they could talk together about His teachings. On this occasion, however, He purposely separated Himself from the twelve. The only way for Him to be alone was to plan His day and to make the circumstances compatible with His will. Because the twelve always pressed for His time and attention, He sent them away in order to have seasons alone with the Father. After dismissing the multitude, He carried through with His plan to have a Quiet Time. He went up on the mountain and spent the evening in prayer. He was in control of His life.

Mark wrote, "And when it was evening, the boat was in the midst of the sea, and He was alone on the land. And seeing them straining at the oars, for the wind was against them, at about the fourth watch of the night, He came to them, walking on the sea; and He intended to pass by them." [27] We are all familiar with the miracle of His walking on the water as He crossed the Sea of Galilee, but have you ever stopped to consider the reason He did it? Every activity of that late afternoon and night was calculated to serve His purpose. The Lord did not walk on water as a public miracle to be gazed at. He even intended to pass His own disciples by. The one and only reason this miracle was necessary was the supreme importance He attached to being alone in prayer. You and I cannot walk on water to have a Quiet Time, but we can make provision for being alone with God as Jesus did.

How can we follow His example in today's world? For starters, we can cut the radio off in the car and use travel time for prayer and meditation. We can listen to cassettes of the Bible while walking or jogging, call a moratorium on excessive TV viewing, and create an atmosphere of quiet in our lives. Much of man's noise is a form of escapism by which he attempts to fill his loneliness. For the Christian, islands of quiet are times for listening, planning, fellowship, and peace of mind.

The great decisions of Jesus were normally made during these private times. His twelve apostles were chosen after a full night of prayer.[28] And the greatest victory of His life was accomplished in solitary agony as He said, "Not what I will, but what You will"![29] If it had not been for the triumph at Gethsemane, there would have been no Calvary.

Ultimately, the forgiveness of our sins was made possible as the result of Jesus' unfailing commitment to carve islands in His day for prayer. It was through this practice that He lived in unbroken obedience and perfect fellowship with the Father and the wisdom He needed was provided. That same provision is available for each one of us. James says, "If any of you lacks wisdom, let him ask of God, who gives to all men generously. . . ."[30] If we fail to take advantage of this provision, it is simply an evidence that we "have not" because we "ask not."[31]

Who will suffer if we fail to carve islands in our day? If Jesus had failed, He would have forfeited His destiny, but we would have been the ones to suffer. The same concept holds true today. If we fail to listen, we forfeit our ministry, but those we could have reached for Christ will pay the greatest price for our spiritual indifference.

PRINCIPLE #5: *Put Others First*

The Scripture says, "Do for others what you want them to do for you."[32] With that Golden Rule in mind, let's pose a question: what if you were depending upon someone like you to explain the plan of salvation to you? What would be the likelihood of your learning how to go to heaven? Would you want their prayer life of intercession on your behalf to be like yours? Would you want their discipline and knowledge of the Bible to resemble yours? How about their love? Would you want their level of concern for your eternal destiny to be equated with the burden you have for others?

If your honest answers to these questions are "No," then you will understand why God wants to produce major changes in the quality of your life. People mattered to Jesus. For this reason, He strove to be everything they needed. He said, "I have come not to be ministered unto but to minister." [33] He reminded us that a student is not above his teacher.[34] He showed us how to bear witness at every turn in life by reaching down to the defeated, like the woman at the well,[35] and challenging intellectuals, like Nicodemus.[36] We are called to do the same.

If you were a greedy swindler like Zacchaeus, a leader like Lazarus, a man of wealth like Joseph of Arimathea, a rebel like Paul, a common fisherman like Peter, a timid teenager like John Mark, an immoral woman like Mary Magdalene, or a tender woman of faith like Mary of Bethany [37]—how would you want to be treated? Would you want someone to share the Gospel of Christ with you?

As we look at the several billion who populate our world and consider the small percentage who have received Christ as their Lord and Savior, this question becomes extremely personal. Put yourself in their position—confused, lonely, or even bitter. At best, they have a caricature of what God might be like. Living without Christ, their minds are focused on things that are material. Paul says, "Those who live as their human nature tells them to, have their minds controlled by what human nature (flesh) wants. . . ." [38] This results in spiritual death.

Jesus said, "I have come that they might have life, and that they might have it more abundantly." [39] Because people were His purpose for coming to earth, as He lives through us they will become our purpose as well.

The apostle Paul explains how we learn to put people first when he declares, "For it is God which worketh in you both to will and to do of His good pleasure." [40]

If you want to live in victory, the ultimate means for this adventure is Christ Himself. No list of principles, however true they may be, will ensure the quality of life which you desire. But be assured that victory is yours for the taking, because the One who lives in you is victorious. Rely upon Him to live out His resurrected life—through you. He is more than adequate for every trial and opportunity in your future. As you review these five principles, decide to let Him live them out through you on a daily basis.

6
Adoration

Bless the Lord, O my soul: and all that is within me, bless his holy name. (*Psalm 103:1, KJV*)

When considering the person of God, the Psalmist declared: "How great is Thy goodness . . !" [1] Many centuries later, the hymnwriter, Stuart K. Hine, perhaps contemplating this same truth, wrote some of the world's most beloved lyrics:

> O Lord my God! When I in awesome wonder
> Consider all the worlds * Thy hands have made,
> I see the stars, I hear the rolling * thunder,
> Thy power throughout the universe displayed,
> Then sings my soul, my Savior God to Thee:
> How great Thou art, How great Thou art!

Since earliest times, man has stood in awe of the majesty and wonder of God and His power, as revealed in creation. But it

---

is in the Bible that we come to understand the personal nature of God's love and His involvement with those who believe in Him.

Moses witnessed God's powerful protection as plague after plague was sent against the mighty army of Egypt. With each miracle the ancient world was drawn to a deeper respect for Jehovah God. At last the children of Israel, who had long been in bondage, were set free. They were led by a pillar of fire by night and a special cloud during the day. The sea opened before them, allowing safe passage to freedom, and it closed behind them, destroying that era's mightiest army on earth. Their sandals withstood the torturous elements; food and water were supplied in abundance in the wilderness. In addition, God audibly spoke to Moses and showed him the glowing beauty and awesome power of His presence.[2]

Moses understood more about God than any man who had ever lived prior to his day, yet even he was aware that he had only *begun* to understand God's greatness. In the last days of his life, at the ripe old age of 120, he prayed earnestly to the Lord, saying, "O Lord God, Thou hast *begun* to show Thy servant Thy greatness and Thy strong hand . . . who can do such works and mighty acts as Thine?"[3]

Communicating Love for God

Adoration is expressed in many ways because of our various personalities and gifts. Because we feel love, we want to communicate it. Ultimately the language of the heart will find its highest expression in talking with God about Himself. This unique kind of prayer is called Adoration. Through it, we praise God for *who* He is. The more you learn about Him, the more you will understand how little you really know! The joy of that continuing discovery and loving mystery causes us to live in a sense of expectation. This is much deeper than simply praying a prayer.

Few Christians have a crisp, clear understanding of this subject. They tend to confuse adoration with thanksgiving. When we thank God for *what* He does, we are gratefully recognizing His answers to our *petitions*. Adoration, on the other hand, focuses on God Himself rather than the things He does.

The Psalmist said, "O Lord, our Lord, How majestic is Thy

name in all the earth." [4] But I would guess that only a small percentage of a thousand unrehearsed prayers will be expressions of adoration. How often do you hear a person pray, "Lord, You are faithful. Your love is everlasting. Your wisdom is perfect. What an honor it is to be Your child"?

You may be saying, "I don't feel comfortable telling God things like that." Do you remember your first date or the first time you tried to say, "I love you"? Though everything in you knew that to be true, still the words were hard to say. But when they finally came, they meant so much to the one you loved. Adoration is like that. God is waiting for a generation of people who will be shamelessly head-over-heels and openly in love with Him. Why? Is it because God's ego needs to be stroked? No! It's because He knows that we need to learn how to express our love. To say, "God, I love You. You are great!" will not embarrass Him, and it shouldn't embarrass you.

If we infrequently offer prayers of adoration, what kind of praying does receive the majority of our attention? Petition is probably our most frequent form of prayer. While all earnest prayer is pleasing to God, there will be no prayers of petition in heaven, just adoration. We may make requests of God during our time on earth, but throughout eternity, as Christians, we will continue to joyfully speak to God about His glory with words like these: "Thou art worthy, O Lord, to receive glory and honor and power: for Thou hast created all things. . . ." [5] This kind of prayer flows out of your closest moments of fellowship with God. It is the highest form of praise. It is speaking to God from the depths of your heart, letting Him know how much you love Him and how special He is to you.

God cannot be corrupted by our praise. The sin of pride is completely foreign to His character. If you are a parent, His response to our adoration can be easily understood. Our prayers mean as much to Him as sweet words of love mean to you when spoken by your child. He receives them as a blessing. The psalmist says, "I will bless the Lord at all times; His praise shall continually be in my mouth." [6] Surely this must be one of the greatest theological mysteries in all the Bible. How is it that you and I can "bless" God? How can small, frail creatures like us be so honored as to bless the infinite Creator?

I've thought about this question many times and I still do

not comprehend the answer, but in some wonderful way when we adore Him it pleases Him. Perhaps it is because our adoration is pre-programmed but an act of free will. Whatever the reason may be, the Bible says that when we sincerely tell God that we love Him and enjoy Him, He appreciates it.

Our Uniqueness

Man was created for the purpose of knowing and loving God. Because we alone are made in His image, we have the privilege of prayer. No other creation in nature has that ability . . . not the tallest tree, the greatest mountain, or the clearest glacier can speak His name. When you express adoration to God you are living out the evidence that you are different from everything else in the universe that He has made.

Among the majestic stars of heaven, the galaxies and myriads of creations, we alone can love God. He made us with the full ability to adore, love, respect and honor Him. Yet, He gave us a will which is free to apply or neglect that sacred ability. Understanding that will have a profound impact on your life. Why? Because those who miss the privilege of loving Him might as well have *never been.* Like a flower that never bloomed, they failed to accomplish their sole purpose in life.

How ironic it is that mankind offers so little adoration, when that is our crowning privilege as human beings. If a person never loves God, he forfeits his divinely given means to inner fulfillment. He is left with a restlessness and a void that no other quality of love can fill.

How to Offer Adoration

If we really love God, we will find a way to express it. One Father's Day, when my older daughter, Heidi, was about 10, I called her long distance and said, "Honey, it's Father's Day, and there is a certain present I would like. Would you be willing to memorize some verses for me as my gift for Father's Day this year?" She said, "Oh, no, Daddy. I can't do that. I have already promised that to the Father for Father's Day." I was stunned by her response. The focus of her attention was totally upon God. No one ever told her to give Him a Father's Day present. Her adoration was deeper than words; it was an all-encompassing attitude which found a natural channel of expression.

The words of David, the shepherd boy, appear to be written with effortless sincerity. Psalm 23 affirmed a fact which he knew to be true: the Lord was his shepherd just as surely as he was the shepherd of his own flock. Why do we love that psalm so much? Out of 150 psalms it is perhaps the best known around the world. His attention is not on the sheep, but on the shepherd. *"He* makes me lie down . . . *He* leads . . . *He* restores . . . *He* guides." When David reflects upon the source of his courage, he quickly says, *"Thou* art with me . . . It is *thy* rod and *thy* staff that comfort me." Throughout the passage David is calling our attention to God's faithfulness. Though this psalm is not a prayer in the usual sense of the word, it is nevertheless an unforgettable expression of David's adoration.

We do not have to be able to write like David to achieve this dimension of praise. God gave us the Bible so that in our hearts we can identify with the words of each of its approximately forty inspired authors. In your Quiet Time, through the ministry of the Holy Spirit, you can feel and express the same kind of attitudes and emotions as those who penned the thoughts you are reading.

On a strictly human level, this concept can be seen on Father's and Mother's Days, and on other special occasions when expressions of love are shared through cards written by gifted authors. The words find their meaning in the fact that we have chosen them, not in the fact that we have written them.

In all of history, the foremost example of how to offer adoration was given to us by God rather than man. It was He who taught us the value of praise. When Jesus had reached mature manhood at the age of thirty, it was the Father who publicly expressed adoration for His only Son. When the prophet, John the Baptist, baptized Jesus, a voice from heaven said, "This is My beloved Son, in whom I am well pleased." [7] The Father expressed His adoration in the form of a testimony.

When the Lord taught His disciples to pray, He specifically began with words of adoration for the Father: "Our Father who art in heaven, hallowed be Thy name. Thy kingdom come. Thy will be done, on earth as it is in heaven." [8] It is easy to recognize the majestic quality of praise for God as perfected in Jesus' prayer. That same spirit, that same high exaltation is also present in 1 Chronicles 29:10–11 in the prayer of David. "So, David blessed the Lord in the sight of all the assembly; and David said, 'Blessed art Thou, O Lord God of Israel our father, forever and ever. Thine, O Lord, is the greatness, and the power, and the glory, and the victory, and the majesty, indeed, everything that is in the heavens and the earth; Thine is the dominion, O Lord, and Thou dost exalt Thyself as head over all.' " David blessed the Lord. Typically, in the Hebrew sense, the word *blessed* meant to give a bountiful gift of praise. And David praised his God publicly, in the presence of all the congregation.

Prayers of adoration are not only for our quiet times alone with God; they are also appropriate when groups of Christians gather to worship the Lord. Whether alone or in front of all the people, David prayed with the intensity of one who truly desired to exalt God. The power, the glory, the majesty, the exalted adoration that David ascribed to God, were part of the reason for his affectionate and honored relationship with the Father.

Growing in Adoration

One morning in my Quiet Time I was reading one of David's prayers. I became caught up in the beauty and the majesty of it. The Lord so captivated my thoughts and my spirit through these few verses that I did not want to read any further. I simply wanted to stay there with Him, basking in the light and warmth of that newfound truth. On some mornings in your devotional life, you will not read a whole chapter; you may cover only a few verses, but they will be more than enough to bring you to the point of surrender, worship, and obedience. Don't force the moment. Stay there until God has finished the work He wants to do in your heart.

Quietly listening and allowing the Holy Spirit to help you visualize what the Scriptures describe will enhance and intensify the quality of your adoration.

Consider Paul's words to the early Christians who lived in the city of Colossae. In describing the Lord Jesus, he said, "And He is the image of the invisible God, the first-born of all creation.

For by Him all things were created, both in the heavens and on earth, visible and invisible, whether thrones or dominions or rulers or authorities—all things have been created by Him and for Him. And He is before all things, and in Him all things hold together." [9] These three powerful sentences rank among the most important in all the Scriptures. The one true God, who has been invisible to man, intentionally became visible once in human history. This is worthy of our total concentration.

As a president's wife or a queen holds the title of first lady of the land, Christ, in His humanity, holds the sacred title of the *first born* or most pre-eminent of all creation. Not only do we honor him as God, but since He chose to become a man we honor Him supremely in the human realm as well. Paul wrote that "everything, everywhere was created by Him and for Him." The entire universe and spiritual realms which man does not begin to understand are all His handiwork. Should it come as a surprise that awe and wonder frequently accompany our adoration when we come before the Living Christ in prayer? His name is above every name and the Scriptures declare that ultimately "at the name of Jesus every knee shall bow, of those who are in heaven, and on earth, and under the earth, and that every tongue shall confess that Jesus Christ is Lord, to the glory of God the Father." [10]

As strange as it may seem, the vilest sinner, the cynical atheist, the most egotistical philosopher, and every other nonbeliever will join God's prophets and Christian saints offering prayers of adoration to the Lord Jesus Christ. Those who are saved will do this from the glory of heaven but the lost will do it from their chosen estrangement in hell. Adoration will be the universal experience of every human being who has ever lived. It will express the utter joy of the wise and the crushing disappointment of the fool.

Limitless Riches

Try to see what Paul is describing in this passage written to the Christians in Rome: "Oh, the depth of the riches both of the wisdom and knowledge of God! How unsearchable are His judgments and unfathomable His ways! For who has known the mind of the Lord, or who became His counselor?" [11] How much would world leaders and educational institutions gladly give to obtain and understand the wisdom of God!

The truth Paul expressed many centuries ago is timeless. There is no end to the riches of God's wisdom and knowledge. All that contemporary society could give would not begin to compare with the value of these divine attributes. His decisions and choices are perfect and, though we may search and try our best to understand them, this side of heaven some will remain mysteries to us. This is why God has said that "without faith it is impossible to please Him, for he who comes to God must believe that He is, and that He is a rewarder of those who seek Him." [12]

Seeking God and desiring to know Him more deeply is the lifelong pursuit of every Christian. We look backward to the occasion when we were forgiven and cleansed. We look forward to Christlikeness and the privilege of increased service and understanding. Throughout this journey, adoration is to be our constant companion.

"And though you have not seen Him, you love Him, and though you do not see Him now, but believe in Him, you greatly rejoice with joy inexpressible and full of glory"! [13]

To explore the joys of adoration on a morning-by-morning basis, you will want to make use of the prayer section of the sample *Spiritual Journal* located in the Appendix. When you encounter verses in your daily Quiet Time like Psalm 9:2b, "I will sing praise to Thy name, O Most High," stop and sing a hymn or chorus of praise to the Lord. Some examples would be "All Hail the Power of Jesus' Name," "O Come, All Ye Faithful," "The Lamb Is Worthy," "A Mighty Fortress," or "How Great Thou Art." When you read Psalm 8:9, "O Lord, our Lord, How majestic is Thy name in all the earth!" stop reading long enough to tell the Father how holy and exalted He is to you. Let him know how proud you are to bear the name, Christian. When you read a verse, like, "Blessed be the God and Father of our Lord Jesus Christ, who . . . has caused us to be born again . . .",[14] pause to bless Him yourself, giving Him praise for the fact that you have been gloriously born into the family of God.

7
Petition

. . . in everything by prayer and supplication with thanksgiving let your requests be made known unto God. (Philippians 4:6b, KJV)

A Great Invitation

God has petitioned us to make petitions. He said, "Call to Me, and I will answer you, and I will tell you great and mighty things, which you do not know." [1] This is an amazing invitation coupled with an equally amazing promise. Toward the end of Jesus' earthly ministry, He encouraged His disciples with these words: "Until now you have asked for nothing in My name; ask, and you will receive, that your joy may be made full." [2]

Because of God's love and the disciples' belief that Jesus had come "forth from the Father," [3] a wonderful *change* in their prayer life was about to take place. This would occur when they would see Him again after His crucifixion and resurrection. [4] At that time, He would no longer speak to them using parables and allegories but would teach them in simplest words about the Father and His kingdom. By then they would be ready to better understand the deep truths He wanted to communicate.

Praying in the Name of Jesus Christ

After His resurrection, there would be no further need for Jesus to humanly make requests of the Father on their behalf. Those who believed in Him would be able to go directly to the Father offering their petitions in His name.[5]

This was a new teaching. For centuries, Hebrew believers had prayed to Jehovah God based upon their faith, and that faith had been demonstrated by their obedience in offering sacrifices at the Temple in Jerusalem. But now the Father was providing the *timeless* and *sinless* sacrifice of His only begotten Son, the Lamb of God. From this time forward, all who entered into the forgiveness and cleansing made possible through that sacrifice could go directly to the Father in prayer. How? "In Jesus' name." Why? Because salvation through faith in Christ would open wide the everlasting door of personal *access to* and *fellowship with* God.

Through that perfect sacrifice, the wall of sin separating man and God would at last be removed! The Bible says, "There is no other name under heaven that has been given among men, by which we must be saved." [6] Through faith in Christ, we may now "come boldly unto the throne of grace." [7] All of this and much more was made possible when the Lord ended the Old Testament sacrificial system by giving "His life as a ransom for many." [8] No saint, prophet, or priest in history could have done it, because the life of the Savior had to be *perfect* and *sinless* — as the Bible declares, a "lamb without blemish." [9]

Your prayers sit solidly upon the foundation of Jesus Christ's sinless life, sacrificial death, and victorious resurrection. That is why prayer in His name works!

Understanding the Lord's Promise

Perhaps it startled the Lord's disciples when He said, "If you ask *anything* in My name, I will do it." [10] It sounded as if He were giving them a license to ask for anything they might happen to want. However, some important *prerequisites* were provided for their protection and ours.

Prayer is not like giving a loaded gun to a child. God is fully aware of both our circumstances and the true motives behind our petitions. Referring to the barren results of prayerlessness, the Bible says, "You have not because you ask not." [11] But it also says, "You ask and do not receive, because you ask with wrong motives." [12]

Jesus' early disciples felt the need to pray, so they asked Him to teach them how.[13] Later, when He related their prayers of petition to the fact that the Father would soon be sending the Holy Spirit to indwell them, He said, "He will teach you all things, and bring to your remembrance all that I said to you." [14] Against the background of that promise, Jesus did not hesitate to say, "And whatever you ask in My name, that will I do, that the Father may be glorified in the Son." [15]

If their prayers were based upon the wise instruction of the indwelling Holy Spirit and Jesus' earthly teachings, then their petitions would be the kind God would want to grant. Their prayers would bring glory to the Father.

First Prerequisite

Jesus said, "If you abide in Me, and My words abide in you, ask whatever you wish, and it shall be done for you." [16]

Although the Bible teaches that everyone in the world was created by Christ, the word "if" in this verse makes it clear that abiding in Him is a *choice.* Abiding is descriptive of salvation. The way the Lord used the term, two complementary thoughts are combined—*resting in* because you are *a part of.*

To better understand His use of the word, "abide," consider a tree. A limb rests in the trunk, because it is an integral part of the tree. A Christian rests or abides in Christ because of the spiritual unity which has taken place in the experience of conversion, or what the Bible describes as being "born again." [17] Abiding or resting in salvation is the first prerequisite for answered prayers of petition.

Second Prerequisite

The second prerequisite has to do with Scripture. The Lord said if "My words abide in you." Before you can know how to accomplish His will, you need the guidance of His Word enabling you to pray with understanding. Allowing the Lord's words to abide in you means they are truly at home in your mind, because they have become a part of you.

Jeremiah expressed it this way: "Thy words were found, and I did eat them; and Thy word was unto me the joy and rejoicing of mine heart." [18] He internalized God's word, and it literally became a part of him.

For this to happen to us, Bible reading and Scripture memorization are essential. As we internalize the Scriptures, we come to understand how to pray according to His will. The Bible says, "And this is the confidence which we have before Him, that if we ask anything *according to His will,* He hears us. And . . . we know that we have the requests which we have asked from Him." [19]

Never once were the Lord Jesus' requests denied. Why? Because He prayed according to the Scriptures and always wanted His Father's will.[20] He didn't question it, doubt it, or rebel against it—He did it. This was the key to His unparalleled power in prayer.

Third Prerequisite

A third prerequisite has to do with the attitude of your heart. The Bible says, "Delight yourself also in the Lord; and He will give you the desires of your heart." [21]

Not all of your prayers will be verbalized. Some will remain in the quiet recesses of your thoughts; however, both your spoken and unspoken prayers are important to God. The psalmist said, "Let the *words* of my mouth and the *meditation* of my heart be acceptable in Thy sight, O Lord, my rock and my redeemer." [22]

Because God looks upon your heart, He knows exactly what you desire.[23] Your petitions never escape His notice, and He knows the motivations from which they spring. When He is your delight and His kingdom is what you are seeking, He can trust you with many privileges you would otherwise be unable to enjoy. The Bible says, "No good thing does He (the Lord) withhold from those who walk uprightly." [24]

Your petitions will be denied, however, if your desires are improper. James says, "You ask and do not receive because you ask with the wrong motives." [25]

Why God Sometimes Says "No"

Prayers of petition are exciting because of our sense of expectancy; but there are many occasions when we can thank God that our requests are answered with a "no," rather than a "yes."

At the low water mark in Moses' life, he said, "I cannot carry all these people by myself; the burden is too heavy for me." [26] He had unconsciously shifted the weight of ministry off God's lofty shoulders onto his own. The result was depression, which led to this strange prayer of petition: "If I have found favor in Thy sight, please kill me at once!" [27]

In this unusual petition, Moses presumed to understand his own problem and the best possible solution. It never occurred to him to turn the situation over to God and simply ask Him to take care of it. However, because He fully understood Moses' circumstances, He solved the problem rather than granting his request.

Moses' feelings of inadequacy and frustration were gently lifted when he received an unexpected answer. He was told to share his leadership responsibilities with seventy godly men. The Lord said, "They shall bear the burden of the people along with you, so that you will not have the task alone." [28] God said "no" to Moses' request because of the unfulfilled potential of his life. He did not need to die. He did need to delegate!

How fortunate it is that in God's wisdom our petitions are not always granted. He loves us. He not only listens to our words but responds to the actual need behind our prayers.

When You Don't Know How to Pray

A fable is told about two monks who lived in a monastery hidden high in the mountains. Each was given the responsibility of caring for a seedling pine tree. They decided to compare the growth of their trees one year from the day when they were planted.

When that date finally arrived, one tree had died, while the other was hearty and beautiful. The disheartened monk with the lifeless tree came to discuss the matter with his colleague, producing a long list of dated petitions he had offered for his tree. The list included sunshine on some days, rain on others, and protection from insects and specific diseases. He had even asked for wind, frost, and snow to strengthen the little tree's endurance.

Curious to know what he had done wrong, he was eager to see the other monk's list. To his surprise, he had none! His daily petition had been a simple prayer in which he said, "Lord, You know that I am unsuited for the responsibility of caring for this little tree. But You also know its every need, because You created it. So please make it grow for Your glory."

The moral to this story is worth remembering: When in doubt about how to pray, pray anyway and trust your need to God, allowing *Him* to determine the answer. There is no circumstance beyond His knowledge, and there is no need too small or too large for His care.

The Bible says, "Don't worry about anything; instead, pray about everything; tell God your needs and don't forget to thank him for his answers." [29]

A "No" from God Means a "Yes" to Something Better

I drive a Chevrolet Suburban, but my heart has always belonged to sports cars. You can imagine my thrill when my parents and grandmother called my university dorm years ago to say they had bought me a beautiful used gold Corvette. It had the biggest engine available and a four-speed transmission that almost caused the car to jump in first and second gears.

As soon as I hung up the phone, I felt impelled to pray. I petitioned, "Father, I'm so grateful for this car, but I just want to double-check whether or not You really want me to have it." I had never consciously prayed for a Corvette, but God knew how badly I had wanted one!

A question came to mind as I offered my prayer for guidance: "Do you love your Sunday school class?" And I answered, "I sure do." My class of corner newspaper salesmen and shoeshine boys was an informal but regular group of seven. I picked them up every Sunday morning in my Valiant station wagon. God spoke to my heart, "Billie, how do you think you are going to get all those kids in that little Corvette?"

"Well, I could take off the top and let them hang out!"

God made it very clear as I prayed that I must decide whether ministry to people or the love of things was going to be the overriding principle in my life. I was fearful of disappointing my parents and my grandmother, but to my surprise they gladly affirmed my decision. In fact, they allowed me to choose a new, more expensive Pontiac that had "four on the floor" and three two-barrel carburetors—but it was big enough to hold plenty of boys. Soon a caravan of three cars was required to handle the growth of the class!

God's "no" to the sports car was not a "no" to fun or beauty. It was simply His means of giving me a "yes" to something safer, better, and more usable at that stage of my life.

How to Pray in the Hard Times

Ultimately, in every person's experience there comes a time to ask the question, "How do I pray in this most difficult situation?" Recently I wrote a letter to a concerned husband who needed an answer to that question. His beloved wife was critically ill with cancer. What kind of petition should he bring to God in this circumstance?

A mature prayer would be: "Lord, I love the precious wife You have given me, and I thank You for being with her during this time of great need. I ask that You bring glory to Yourself through this difficult experience. If this can be accomplished by healing her, please do it, and I will thank You with all my heart. But if it will bring You greater glory to take her to Yourself, then please give me the strength to serve You and praise You when she is gone. I do not doubt Your love for her, nor Your power to heal her. Father, I know that our best interest is always on Your heart and that You will make no mistake in this matter. So whether she lives or whether she dies, let our witness be the kind that will bring others to faith in Christ."

Where is the mature faith in this prayer? It is found in these words: "I know that our best interest is always on Your heart and that You will make no mistake in this matter." Knowing that hard times would come, the Lord made this promise: "Fear not, for I am with you; be not dismayed, for I am your God. I will strengthen you. Yes, I will help you, I will uphold you with My righteous right hand." [30]

The measure of maturity in one's petitions does not have to

do with the *size* of the request—for with God *nothing* is impossible.[31] He is not impressed by a loud voice, a tone of authority, or the scope of our petition. What pleases Him is the nature of our prayer. When we love Him enough to desire His glory more than deliverance from our temporary inconvenience or hardship, it brings Him great joy.

Nowhere is this more clearly demonstrated than in the prayers of Jesus. When He was agonizing in the Garden of Gethsemane and preparing for His most difficult hour, He said, "Father, if you are willing, take this cup from me; yet not my will, but yours be done." [32] Which would bring God the greater glory: for Jesus to be delivered from Calvary or for Him to go through Calvary? The adversity of the cross was the gateway to victory. Without the crucifixion, there could be no resurrection!

You will be most like Jesus when the preoccupation of your life is glorifying your heavenly Father. It was the Savior who prayed, "I have glorified you on the earth. I have finished the work which You have given Me to do." [33]

The Principle of Victory

Few men in history have understood as much about effective prayer as the apostle Paul. The book of Acts is filled with "yes" answers to Paul's requests; however, in one notable instance God said, "No." Paul wrote the Christians in Corinth about his prayers concerning a physical infirmity which he described as a "thorn in the flesh." He said, "I entreated the Lord three times that it might depart from me, and He has said to me, 'My grace is sufficient for you, for My power is perfected in weakness.' " [34]

When Paul went to Galatia to preach the Gospel, it is clear that he arrived with a physical infirmity. At a later date, he reminded them of this fact, saying, "It was because of a bodily illness that I preached the gospel to you the first time; and that which was a trial to you in my bodily condition you did not despise or loathe. . . . If possible, you would have plucked out your eyes and given them to me. . . ." [35]

It is obvious that Paul's problem had continued, since he concluded his letter by saying, "See with what large letters I am writing to you." [36] At that point, he took the pen from his secretary and wrote these words himself to prove the authenticity of the letter.

Although the great apostle had been the instrument through whom God had healed many others, in this instance it was not God's will for him to be healed. If Paul could heal himself or others *at will*, you can imagine the temptation toward pride. But if he had to leave Trophimus, his friend, sick at Miletus[37] and could not heal himself, he would constantly be reminded of his total dependence on God.

Because the Lord wanted to protect Paul from exalting himself, He intentionally left him with this infirmity.[38] Once Paul understood that God could work through him with greater spiritual power if he remained in physical weakness, the victory was won. He rejoiced saying, "Most gladly, therefore, I will rather boast about my weaknesses, that the power of Christ may dwell in me [39] . . . for when I am weak, then I am strong." [40]

This principle was vividly illustrated again when Paul and Silas were harshly beaten with rods and placed in stocks in the Philippian jail. The two men sat there bleeding while singing and praising God. It was for God's glory that they remained in pain until after the doors were miraculously opened, and they went to their jailer's house. There the repentant Gentile jailer mercifully cleansed their backs and washed their wounds. Because of their testimony, an entire family was saved that night.[41] It was through physical suffering that God was glorified.

Was that the kind of answer you expected or wanted the last time you offered a petition? Probably not! Our human nature recoils at the suggestion that suffering, pain, financial reverses, or the loss of something dear to us could be good.

It is only with maturity that we come to understand Paul's words that "all things work together for good to those who love God." [42] If he had not experienced hunger, criticism, stonings, beatings, shipwrecks, imprisonment, and disappointment,[43] perhaps those words would sound idealistic. But from his lips they are nothing less than a challenge for all Christians to live above their circumstances and experience inward victory.

When God Says "Yes"

Those who keep prayer lists have long since discovered that the overwhelming majority of their prayers are answered with a "yes." If the multitude of divine "yes" answers could be cataloged, it is doubtful that any computer ever made could contain them. From the first prayer ever prayed until now, the number would be staggering, because millions of God's children bring their small and large petitions to Him daily.

For the one time when God said "no" to Moses' request to take his life, there were scores of times when God positively answered his prayers for protection and guidance. En route to the promised land of Canaan, God's children received a constant succession of "yeses." With the slavery of Egypt behind them and the promise of milk, honey, and freedom ahead of them, they still faced all the obstacles which a barren wilderness affords.

As Moses sought God's direction, he said, "I pray, if I have found grace in Your sight, show me now Your way. . . ." [44] God's immediate and comforting answer is typical of His response to our own petitions as we seek to do His will. He said, "My presence shall go with you, and I will give you rest." [45] Moses wanted to know His way but received even more than he asked for. God not only wants to show us His way, but to personally walk with us in those blessed paths. Beyond that, He also promises rest on the journey.

Knowing how God feels about you as His child should be your greatest motivation for bringing Him your petitions in faith. He wants to say "yes," and your petitions are invited. What greater reason could you have for expressing your needs and desires to Him throughout the day.

As you bring your petitions to God, seeking His will, you can *expect* a "yes" but by faith must be equally willing to *accept* a "no." This quality of prayer is best achieved by spending time in the Scriptures and meditating upon what you read and hear. This will enable His words to "abide in you." Remember, you have been instructed to "let your requests be made known to God," [46] with this promise: That "the peace of God, which surpasses all understanding, will guard your hearts and minds through Christ Jesus." [47]

8
Confession

Unconfessed sin is like spoiled food in the pantry, dirt in the living room, or anything else which degrades its surroundings. It is totally out of character with a redeemed life!

Because we are still imperfect even after our conversion experience, confession is the norm, but ever-increasing purity in thought and deed is our constant goal. Living in compromise with, or harboring, sin in our hearts is unacceptable and unbecoming in God's children.

The sins of pride, lust, greed, lying, bitterness, or a lack of faith, have the same negative effect on the life of a believer that they have on an unbeliever. However, there is one important exception: A Christian is assured of forgiveness and knows how to claim that promised help. The Bible says, "If we confess our sins, He is faithful and just to forgive us our sins, and to cleanse us from all unrighteousness." [1]

Unconfessed sin takes away the joy of our salvation and the dignity that accompanies a committed Christian's life. Lack of confession can be equated with a life of spiritual mediocrity, or what the Bible calls "carnality." It can produce depression, feelings of guilt, discouragement, lack of assurance, and a host of other symptoms which erode the wonderful pleasure of living.

For this reason, confession is one of the most liberating kinds of prayer you will ever experience. The psalmist describes God's desire for our confession and cleansing when he says, ". . . A broken and a contrite heart, O God, you will not ignore." [2]

He desires our prayers of confession because of our need, but such prayers would never have to be prayed if it were not for the problem of sin, so we need to answer the questions, "What is sin? And where does it come from?"

What Is Sin?

In a broad sense, there are only two kinds of sin. The best-understood is the *sin of commission.* Paul defines this form in 1 John 3:6: "Sin is the transgression of the law." [3] This means willfully breaking the Ten Commandments or doing what you *know* to be wrong.

I vividly remember my first conscious decision to do this. I was just a little boy, but I understood exactly what I was doing. One warm summer afternoon I saw two glistening green Coke bottles which belonged to the Johnsons, our next-door neighbors. For some reason, the bottles looked as appealing to me as emeralds would to an adult. A very real battle took place within my mind. It was as if Satan and God were each stating their case. I knew inwardly it was wrong to steal. For what seemed an eternity, I paced up and down the driveway separating our houses. Then I willfully chose to become a thief and ran to get the Coke bottles as fast as I could.

As soon as I crossed the driveway headed home, the full impact of my decision struck me. Suddenly the bottles in my hands lost all their glamor. I can distinctly recall a feeling I had never experienced before. It was as if something wonderful had died! Immediately I told God I was sorry and took the Coke bottles back, placing them behind the bush by the porch where I had found them. That painful experience was followed by other willful, sinful decisions which finally led me to admit my need of a Savior.

The other category of sin is described by James, "Knowing what is right to do and then not doing it is sin." [4] This is generally called the *sin of omission.*

God expressed His disdain for this kind of sin when He asked,

" 'Will a man rob God? Surely not! And yet you have robbed me.' 'What do you mean? When did we ever rob you?' 'You have robbed me of the tithes and offerings due to me . . . Bring all the tithes into the storehouse so that there will be food enough in my Temple; if you do, I will open up the windows of heaven for you and pour out a blessing so great you won't have room enough to take it in! Try it! Let me prove it to you!' " [5]

The omission of giving 10 percent of your income back to the Lord is as sinful as embezzling an extra 10 percent from the business where you work. Once you understand this, you will see why so much is said in the Bible about the importance of stewardship. Giving is not only a command, but a tangible expression of our love. Jesus said, "If you love Me, keep My commandments." [6]

The sin of omission reflects an irresponsible attitude, and the Bible says, "Do not withhold good from those who deserve it, when it is in your power to act." [7] It is always a Christian's responsibility to do what is right.

The overall teaching of the Bible with regard to sin is best summarized in the words of Paul, who said, ". . . whatsoever is not of faith is sin." [8] What does this mean? If on the basis of God's Word you question the validity of an act, but you do it anyway, you are not acting in faith. On the contrary, you are acting out of doubt. This means that you are proceeding on your own without praying and waiting for God's clear leading.

A tragic decision in the life of King Saul vividly demonstrates the meaning of this verse. He was told to go to a certain place and wait seven days for the prophet Samuel, who would prepare a special offering to sacrifice to the Lord.[9] But when Saul saw that the crowd gathered for the worship service was beginning to scatter, he became uncertain of what to do and took matters into his own hands. In direct disobedience to God's instruction, he personally offered the sacrifice which the prophet Samuel was to have made. Had Saul responded in faith rather than fear, he would have obeyed God in spite of the outward circumstances. His vacillating obedience brought forth a strong rebuke from God and caused him to lose his position of leadership.

This is an extreme example, but it underscores two important principles. First, when God gives you something to do, the outward circumstances will not always make it convenient to obey.

When Jesus redeemed us, He experienced adversity and pain, but by faith He was obedient, even to the point of dying on a cross. If He had chosen the easy road rather than the path of faith, He would have failed in His divine mission. The same is true for us.

Second, a high percentage of life's mistakes are brought about by impatience. If Saul had asked the Lord for guidance and taken time to pray, how different his life would have been. It is important to remember that God is more interested in showing us His will than we are in finding it. If He says "go," go in faith! If He says "stop," stop in faith! If He doesn't say, *wait* in faith!

Paul said, "The just shall live by faith." [10] When we seek to do that, we are protected from sins of commission and omission.

Where Does Sin Come From?

Above anything else, it must be said that sin does not come from God. The Bible says, "Let no one say when he is tempted, 'I am being tempted by God'; for God cannot be tempted by evil, and He Himself does not tempt anyone. But each one is tempted when he is carried away and enticed by his own lust. Then when lust has conceived, it gives birth to sin. . . ." [11]

When James says we are enticed by our *own lusts,* he is talking about the fallen nature of man. Since the earliest times, man has had an independent and often rebellious spirit. This is why Paul says, "all have sinned and fall short of the glory of God." [12]

As a guest preacher in a small Western town, a close friend of mine was invited to stay in a private home. When morning came, he ate breakfast with a boy named Johnny, who was considered the "terror" of the neighborhood. As they ate, while his mother's back was turned, the boy picked up his bowl of cereal and milk and threw it upside down on the table. Much of it landed on my friend's good suit. Trying to comfort the mother in a very awkward situation, he said, "It's all right. That could have happened to anyone. I'll put on my other suit and be right back." When he returned he looked at the little boy as if to say, "You wouldn't!" But as soon as the mother turned her back, Johnny did it again! The mother was so unnerved she began to cry. Can you imagine hosting a visiting minister and having your child throw milk and cereal on him—twice? Realizing it wasn't an accident, the mother walked over to the table and asked, "Johnny, why did you do that?" Defiantly, the little boy looked up and said, "Mother, *I do as I please!*"

Down through the ages, man has glared at God in defiance saying, "I will do whatever I please." The Scripture says, "The heart is deceitful above all things, and desperately wicked." [13] It is the source of our self-will! Though he didn't know it, when little Johnny expressed his selfish feelings, they were coming from his heart. Jesus expressed this truth when He said, "For out of the abundance of the heart the mouth speaks." [14]

In the final analysis, all sin is the result of the *self-will* which resides in the human heart. This is why no lasting change can take place in your life until Christ is enthroned as Lord in that domain!

Turning over a new leaf is inadequate in dealing with sin. Why? Because our outward acts are only symptoms of the deeper problem within. The Bible says, "From the heart come evil thoughts, murder, adultery, fornication, theft, lying, and slander." [15] This is why David cried out to God in confession after his tragic sin with Bathsheba, saying, "Create in me a clean heart, O God; and renew a right spirit within me." [16] He knew the source of his sin.

Jesus enlarged upon this truth when He explained that, "Anyone who even looks at a woman with lust in his eye has already committed adultery with her in his heart." [17] This is why the Bible says, "Keep your heart with all diligence, for out of it spring the issues of life." [18]

Confession and Repentance

Confession is admitting that you have chosen to do your will rather than God's. Repentance involves trusting God to change your heart as you willfully choose not to sin again.

Jesus' contemporary and cousin, John the Baptist, preached this message with biting practicality. When previously hypocritical religious leaders came to be baptized, He warned them to "bring forth fruit in keeping with repentance." [19]

What did He mean by this? Sorrow or even verbal admission of our sin is not enough. Although God stands ready and willing to forgive us when we confess, He also requires changed actions, new priorities, and growth in our character. When Jesus forgave, He said, ". . . go, and sin no more." [20]

One evening as we talked in a coffee shop, a friend who was a new Christian asked for some advice about a matter of deep concern. His business partner of seven years had just voluntarily admitted embezzling a large sum of money from their jointly owned company. He was shocked almost beyond belief that his partner had betrayed his trust. Now he was thinking through his alternatives. Should he send the man to the penitentiary or let him go free and try to absorb the loss?

I could see that my friend deeply cared about his unconverted partner and wanted to do whatever was right in terms of the Scriptures. His partner was sorry for what he had done and had voluntarily confessed the crime. What more could he do? The Bible teaches that true confession is always accompanied by repentance. In this case, the evidence of real confession and repentance would be the willingness to repay the stolen money. After our discussion, my friend decided to ask his partner to sign a legally binding note, as if he had *borrowed*, rather than stolen, the money. This would provide him an opportunity to prove his repentance.

To shed light on his own responsibility in the problem, my friend and I discussed the Scriptural injunctions which say, "Don't be teamed with those who do not love the Lord," [21] and "How can a Christian be a partner with one who doesn't believe?" [22] Having never read these verses before, he was shocked to learn that he had violated a very practical biblical principle and was partially responsible for the problem that had developed as a result.

Why Confession Works

A check is of no more value than the bank on which it is written, and forgiveness is available only because the grace of God is adequate to make it possible. If God were spiritually insolvent, confession would be a waste of time. However, the Scripture declares, "God shall supply all your needs according to His riches in glory in Christ Jesus"! [23] When we come to the Father in the name of His Son and our Savior, no matter how big our need might be, we have been assured that His boundless riches are there to make good our request.

How does this work? How can you, on earth, confess a sin in prayer and be assured of God's forgiveness in heaven? Paul explained the answer to that question in his letter to the believers at Corinth: "He (God the Father) made Him (Christ the Son) who knew no sin to be sin on our behalf, that we might become the righteousness of God in Him." [24] This miraculous exchange of guilt, in which Christ bore the full penalty of our sin, is the sole reason confession works. When we confess our sins, we are agreeing with God in two important respects: First, that what we did was not for His glory and was wrong; second, that His grace and power are fully adequate to provide the forgiveness we need.

If Jesus had not been sinless, He could not have been our Savior. One bankrupt person cannot borrow money from another. Describing all mankind, the Bible says, "There is none sinless, no, not one." [25] Speaking of Christ's uniqueness, the Scripture depicts His sinless sacrifice, using the illustration of a priest: "For it was fitting that we should have such a high priest, holy, innocent, undefiled, separated from sinners and exalted above the heavens; who does not need . . . to offer up sacrifices, first for His own sins, and then for the sins of the people, because this He did once for all when He offered up Himself." [26]

Not only is Christ adequate because He is sinless, but because He understands us: "For we do not have a high priest who cannot sympathize with our weaknesses, but one who has been tempted in all things as we are, yet without sin." [27]

He lived His life victoriously, winning every battle on our behalf. The salvation He achieved was effective not only for those who had sought God by faith in the past, but for all who would accept Him as their Savior in the future. He did what no prophet, priest, or king could ever do on man's behalf. Because of His sacrificial death and saving life, confession and its cleansing effect are backed up by all the power and riches of God Himself.

Confession Restores Fellowship

Once while driving down the highway, minding my own business, I was suddenly hit in the head by a hard plastic pink elephant. I had done nothing to provoke it, but it happened anyway. As a result, my daughter and I had a long talk about the fact that there was no excuse for that kind of behavior. While still unrepentant, she received a good spanking. Once she experienced a little of the pain she had inflicted, she understood why hitting people was wrong. Almost immediately her attitude changed, and our fellowship was restored.

She was still my child even though she had hit me in the head with her pink elephant, but our fellowship was clouded until things were straightened out. Sin does not alter our relationship with God, but it does diminish the quality of joy we experience as His child.

We were created for the purpose of fellowship, so when we fail to walk in harmony with God, we bring Him little pleasure. Unconfessed sin hinders our fellowship with Him, because it creates a barrier in our prayer life, and prayer is our means of spiritual communication. Understanding this fact, the psalmist said, "He would not have listened if I had not confessed my sins." [28]

Your relationship with Christ is eternal; it is solid and stable. You love Him, and He loves you, but confession of sin is necessary in order to maintain the normal joy and quality of that relationship.

Confessing to One Another

Having looked at the vertical aspects of confession between you and God, there is another dimension that needs to be considered. You are also told to "confess your sins one to another, and pray for one another." [29] The spirit of this teaching was made clear by the Lord when He delivered His famous Sermon on the Mount. He said, "Therefore if you bring your gift to the altar, and there remember that your brother has something against you, leave your gift there before the altar, and go your way. First be reconciled to your brother, and then come and offer your gift." [30]

Confessing a bad attitude or asking forgiveness for an act committed against your brother is even more important to God than your prayer of confession. Why is this true? Because character development and honesty are more important to God than mere words. He is constantly looking for change as the evidence of your spiritual growth.

When you have your Quiet Time, be specific in relating every prayer of confession to a tangible change which you want to see in your life. Relate that change to the sin you are confessing.

Never confess with the secret intent of committing that sin again. Always plan for spiritual improvement, and God will honor your faith with the strength to say "no" to temptation and "yes" to righteousness. Paul said, "I can do all things through Christ who strengthens me." [31]

9
Thanksgiving

Let us come before His presence with thanksgiving. (Psalm 95:2a)

Can Christians thank God in all circumstances? Yes! Because "we know that all things work together for good to those who love God, to those who are the called according to His purpose." [1] We can thank Him for that truth, especially in our darkest and loneliest hours. He is not afraid of hard times and promised, "I will never leave you nor forsake you." [2] One of the names used to describe our Lord is Immanuel. It means—God with us! And He always is.

You are never alone. In your highest moments of inspiration and the heaviest hours of your grief, He is with you. You are not a victim of your circumstances. The Lord said, "In this world you will have trouble. But take heart! I have overcome the world." [3]

Thanksgiving is living in the very heart of *reality*. It is a reality that defies explanation outside our relationship with Christ. Those around you who do not know Christ are living outside of reality and are blind to the principles and resources the Lord made available to us when He overcame the world. This is why the Christian's optimism is often thought of as naive. It also explains why we often see society's values as selfish, cynical, and arbitrary.

Thanksgiving is based upon facts that cannot be changed and truth that brings light into darkness. The angel whose words we sing at Christmas said, "I bring you good news of a great joy . . . for today in the city of David there has been born for you a Savior." [4] From that time until our time, the lives of those who have met the Savior have been seasoned with joy and thanksgiving.

Jesus' Attitude toward Thankfulness

From the beginning of Christ's earthly ministry, He looked for the attribute of thanksgiving in the lives of people. One day, as He and the disciples walked "toward Jerusalem, they reached the border between Galilee and Samaria, and as they entered a village there, ten lepers stood at a distance, crying out, 'Jesus, sir, have mercy on us!' He looked at them and said, 'Go to the Jewish priest and show him that you are healed!' And as they were going, their leprosy disappeared. Only one of them came back to Jesus, shouting, 'Glory to God, I'm healed!' He fell flat on the ground in front of Jesus' face downward in the dust, thanking him for what he had done." [5]

The high value the Lord attached to the words "thank you" is felt in His question to the Samaritan leper whom He had healed, "Were there not ten cleansed? The other nine . . . where are they?" In life, you are either the one who gives thanks or one of the nine who do not. Either you appreciate His daily gifts, or you take them for granted. It is obvious from this passage that God both notices and is moved by our response.

The Lord Jesus was careful to give thanks and to set a proper example for us as God's children. When He fed the 4,000, He gave thanks,[6] and in private with the apostles at their parting meal [7] He did the same. He lived with an attitude of thanksgiving and the awareness that every good and perfect gift comes from the Father.[8]

Biblically, thanksgiving means expressing gratitude to God, not for who He is, but for what He has done. Part of man's sin problem can be clearly seen in his thankless attitude. Paul describes this problem: "Since earliest times men have seen the earth and sky and all God made, and have known of his existence and great eternal power. So they will have no excuse (when they stand before God at Judgment Day). Yes, they knew about him all right, but they wouldn't admit it or worship him or *even thank him for all his daily care.* And after a while they began to think up silly ideas of what God was like and what he wanted them to do. The result was that their foolish minds became dark and confused. . . ." [9]

Barriers to Gratitude

Large blocks of the world's population developed false religions and philosophies which destroyed the very basis for offering sincere thanks to God in prayer. One segment built its religious philosophy around what they call "karma," which simply means "works." Because they believe that their good works produce their blessings, logically they can thank themselves rather than God for all that He gives them. Those religions which believe in fate or chance are equally thankless because there is no one to thank. Who has ever seen or talked with "fate"?

Those who embrace agnosticism or atheism cannot express thanks to anything but nature, and impersonal forces which they do not fully understand. Expressing gratitude with that unrealistic mindset is not only unlikely but illogical.

Lastly, there are those who relentlessly express a form of religious gratitude, but to a god of their own design. Their rigid formalism is expressed with legalistic punctuality. Tragically, such thanksgiving is more like a cuckoo clock, mechanically making the right sounds at the right times. Because the Holy Spirit is not there, the reality of love and a personal relationship with God (which He, too, desires) are absent. As the Apostle Paul taught, lack of thanksgiving is an evidence that true worship is missing.

Beyond man-made religions and philosophies, another barrier to our saying "thank you" seems to be innate in human nature. It is the fear of admitting our own inadequacy. Our unspoken understanding goes like this: "If I have to thank God for something, it means that I cannot do it for myself. Therefore, I must be inadequate." This is true, though our pride makes it extremely hard to accept. We are both physically and spiritually inadequate from the very first days of our lives. Physically, we are born depending upon others and we die depending upon others. To deepen your understanding of this reality, simply visit a hospital nursery and a convalescent home on the same day.

If we who are created in God's image feel the need to hear the words, "thank you," why does it surprise us that He wants to hear those words, as well? If for no other reason, He desires to hear them for our sake, because expressions of appreciation are signs of increasing maturity. When you were a child, at first your parents taught you to say "thank you" whether you felt like it or not. It was only as you matured that the expenditure of other people's effort, time, and material goods became truly significant. A sincere "thank you" is an evidence of growing understanding.

Results of Ingratitude

Ingratitude, on any level, strains a relationship. I personally experienced the sting of ingratitude during my junior year in high school. A houseguest from another country, who had been a casual family acquaintance, wrote asking if he could visit us on his upcoming trip to Texas. He received an enthusiastic "yes" from all of us. To insure his happiness while in San Angelo, it was decided that I would sleep on the couch so he could use my bedroom. In addition, he was to drive my car. Learning of his interest in horses, we arranged for him to ride a good quarterhorse belonging to a neighboring rancher. Other courtesies were planned, including a party honoring him and a trip to Austin to meet the Governor.

His one week stay stretched into two, then three, and finally six! During all this time, our bird-watching, military judo instructor, atheist guest never offered to buy anyone so much as a cup of coffee. However, he did manage to throw me across the living room, wreck the car, and totally lather our friend's horse. More importantly, two words were missing from his otherwise extensive English vocabulary: "Thank you"!

Psalm 24:1 says, "The earth is the Lord's, and all it contains, the world, and those who dwell in it." How embarrassing it would be for otherwise polite people to see themselves as God sees them. They drink His water, eat His food, and enjoy His hospitality to the fullest extent, never realizing that the sky above their heads is His and the grass beneath their feet is the carpet of a beautiful house which belongs to Him. Ironically, He hears His name profaned millions of times every hour, but He seldom hears the words, "Thank you." Even when people are happy or surprised, His name is used as an oath. No human host alive would tolerate such abusive treatment in his own living room.

The opposite of thanksgiving is ingratitude. Ingratitude, carried to its ultimate conclusion, is not only to be unthankful but to rudely ignore the host Himself. The bare beginning of Christian growth is to inwardly feel and express appreciation to your heavenly Host.

When to Say "Thank You"

"In everything give thanks; for this is God's will for you in Christ Jesus." [10] Based upon Paul's words to the early Christians, it is probably more appropriate to ask, "When shouldn't I give thanks?" It is clear that the very attitude of our lives should be one of consistent joy and thanksgiving, regardless of our outward circumstances.

Since Paul was led to pen these words, it is important to know that his walk was consistent with his talk. When he and Silas were imprisoned in Philippi the Scripture says, "They prayed and sang hymns of praise to God" [11] as their fellow prisoners listened. The fact that their feet were in stocks and that they had been beaten with rods earlier in the afternoon did not alter their commitment to giving thanks. Less mature people under similar circumstances would probably have asked, "God, is this how You treat Your best servants?" Instead, Paul and Silas sang and prayed in faith, keeping their focus upon His adequacy in every human situation. When the earthquake came that night and the prison doors swung open, the greater miracle had already occurred within them. They had overcome that tendency of human nature and given praise by faith.

The proper time for an attitude of thanks is—always! But expressing our feelings of gratitude often comes as a result of receiving a new insight. When Nebuchadnezzar, the most powerful man in the world, saw God's miraculous delivery of Shadrach, Meshach, and Abednego, whom Nebuchadnezzar had thrown into a fiery furnace, the king was in awe. He prayed, "Blessed be the God of Shadrach, Meshach, and Abednego, who has sent His angel and delivered His servants who put their trust in Him. . . ." [12] This was an instance where thanksgiving and adoration naturally blended together.

As you pray, this will often occur in your life, as well. In one moment you will be praising God for who He is, and in the next you will be thanking Him for the wonderful things He has done.

What to Be Thankful For

For many years I made the spiritual mistake of taking normal things for granted. But a close friend told me of his experience with the late E. Stanley Jones, one of the best-known missionaries of our century. This godly man shared Christ with great power and clarity throughout much of India.

One day as my friend, Dr. A. B. Masilamani, and Dr. Jones were traveling together, Masi was surprised to see tears in his eyes and asked, "Why are you crying?" "Thanksgiving," said Dr. Jones. "You see, Masi, these legs have carried me up and down the mountains of India for many years, and these hands have been more than faithful in accomplishing what I wanted them to."

Then he thoughtfully patted his knee and complimented it for having worked so well. Thoughtfully, he said, "Before long I will be receiving a new body and be leaving this old friend behind." Little by little, Dr. Jones thanked God for his entire body, one limb at a time.

Most of us never thank God for our eyes, limbs, and ability to function until we have undergone a tragic loss which causes us to appreciate what we had before. May we have the wisdom of this aged saint who, "always giving thanks for all things," [13] thanked God for his body while he still had it. When you start thanking God for normal things, gratitude becomes a way of life. Soon you will become aware of things you have never appreciated before.

Learning what to thank God for really isn't difficult. The key is in understanding that everything you have is provided as a stewardship from Him. This simply means that everything you possess is on loan from God. One businessman has expressed it like this: "We are sharecroppers with a short term lease, operating with money borrowed on a demand note."

Thanking God for Provision

God is watching with great interest to see how you will respond to the privilege of life. The Scripture says if you are faithful in a few things, He will make you ruler over many.[14] Since He is the source of our provision, when He finds our response to be in accordance with His teachings, He can trust us with increased responsibilities and opportunities.

As this relates to material provision, the Lord said, "Seek first the kingdom of God and His righteousness, and all these things shall be added to you." [15] This promise of provision is accompanied by the balance of divine wisdom which is explained in many parts of the Scriptures. When a parent spoils a child or denies him the privilege of learning the value of honest labor, the parent's provision is no longer a blessing but a curse. God's desire is to make us spiritually strong, healthy, and enthusiastic about life. Like any good parent, He must carefully evaluate how many material blessings we need.

You are God's child, and He wants to bless you just as much as you will let Him! He doesn't want to hurt you—He wants to help, and He knows what you need, not what you think you need, even before you ask. Did Jesus not say, ". . . your Father knows what you need, before you ask Him"? [16] The testimony of the psalmist remains ever true, "I have been young, and now I am old; yet I have not seen the righteous forsaken, or his descendants begging bread." [17]

As a seminary student, I learned this important lesson one unforgettable morning in Taiwan. I had been traveling for two months with a team of eight other students, preaching evangelistic crusades around the world. Weeks before, when I left Ruth and our new baby at home, we were still $2,500 short for the overseas ministry, but there was no doubt that the team was supposed to go. In Taiwan, it was quite a shock to discover that each of us thought the others still had some money. It was awkward to share with our missionary host that all we had left was our plane tickets home. At least they would provide meals on the plane!

That morning we prayed that God would give us a definite answer as to whether we should leave immediately or continue with the two exciting weeks of ministry which had been planned. At noon, a cable arrived with the following message: "LETTER TO MAXI JARMAN LOST BY SECRETARY STOP JUST REFOUND STOP SENT $2,500 STOP HE SAID I HOPE IT WILL NOT BE TOO LATE TO BE OF SOME ASSISTANCE STOP."

To say we were thankful would be an understatement. The arrival of the money was not only perfectly timed but his check was for the *exact* remaining need! Our letter to Mr. Jarman had only mentioned the larger amount required for the entire budget. "Faithful is He who calls you, and He also will bring it to pass." [18] God will never call you to carry out a project which He will not staff, empower, and fund!

Thanking God in Times of Stress

Finances are one of God's major ways of dealing with us in spiritual growth, because so much of man's time is devoted to making and spending money. For this reason, some of your greatest tests and most thrilling moments of joy will be related to the possessions which money affords.

A businessman who is a close friend told me how he learned to give thanks in the school of patience. He owned valuable property in a strategic location. Because of his convictions concerning alcoholism, he turned down a substantial offer to build and lease a restaurant which would serve liquor. Then he refused to sell the land for a large eight screen theater which, among other things, would show R-rated films. Like everyone else, he could have used the money, but not at the cost of contributing toward alcoholism or moral decay.

I was not surprised to learn that he was in the midst of negotiating a much better contract using the land for a beneficial purpose. His thanksgiving was accompanied by the peace of mind that comes from letting "patience have its perfect work, that you may be perfect and complete, lacking nothing." [19]

Health either has been or will be an important area for thanksgiving in your life. Sometimes the occasion for joy is for yourself, and sometimes on behalf of others. In either case, as the Scripture says, "It is good to give thanks to the Lord." [20]

It is hard to imagine giving thanks for mononucleosis, but Ruth and I have learned that there are times when you can almost shout for joy over such a diagnosis. Our oldest daughter, Heidi, had not been well for over six months. She had been to several doctors and had had a bone scan, a brain scan, and an encephalogram. The doctors had prepared us for the worst, because they feared the diagnosis would be epilepsy, a brain tumor, or multiple sclerosis. Heidi had subconsciously committed herself to get ready to "leave for heaven." The final straw (and answer too!) was an alarming swelling on both sides of her neck. That was the clue the doctors needed to order a simple blood test which confirmed an unusual and long-lasting form of mononucleosis.

Though she had to miss an overseas trip, on which she had been invited to play the harp with the Youth Orchestra, she fully shared our joy and thanked God for these circumstances. For her, giving thanks was an evidence of growing maturity in her faith. For us, it was sheer appreciation for His guidance which we had earnestly sought as parents.

Take Time to Listen

Some years ago, I felt there was a need for a certain kind of Christian music. With little or no specific prayer, I dove into the project. After six months of diligent effort, the manuscript was ready to mail to a potential publisher.

In anticipation of calling a music publisher in Chicago, I went to my bedroom for a time of private prayer. In retrospect, it is clear that my attitude could not have pleased God, because there was no real adoration for Him in my heart—only adoration for the music. My words sounded pious as I reminded Him that His name was mentioned throughout the music and that the songs were dedicated in His honor.

Prayer is a spiritual dialogue, and in our minds God is faithful to carry out His part of the conversation. The key is stopping to listen. On this occasion, the communication was unmistakably clear: "Billie, you say the music belongs to Me. If it does, you won't care what I choose to do with it, will you?"

My immediate reaction was one of puzzlement. I began to gently argue my position: "Lord, wouldn't You like to bless the music for Your glory and make it sell thousands of copies?" This was the beginning of a painful six-week struggle, during which I was aware that I could not call Chicago and be in God's will until I was fully prepared to thank Him equally for a "yes" or "no" answer from the publisher.

Only when my focus turned away from the music, and only when His will became more important to me than my aspirations, did the victory come. The music was never published.

Years later, I found the manuscript in a drawer. Curiously, I re-read the words of each song, and thanked God again—this time for a different reason. The music was so shallow and faddish that it was totally unworthy of bearing His name!

The deeper lesson that came from this experience has been of genuine benefit ever since. The objective of the Christian life is living in the kind of obedience that demonstrates our love. We are not to set out on projects of our own and then ask God to bless them. He will never rubber stamp our will. However, when music or anything else is born in heaven and He commissions us to move in a certain direction, the simplest obedience will be accompanied by amazing results.

This reminds me of an incident that occurred while I was serving as a youth evangelist. Ruth and I had been praying that God would enable us to increase our giving for His work. Our five dollars a week seemed such a small tithe in view of the tremendous needs throughout the world. The Lord's response to that prayer was to ask me to give Him something with the stipulation that I would never personally use any of the income which might be derived from that gift. What He wanted, and what I gave Him that day, was a song which had been written out of a haunting concern for the loneliness of lost people in huge urban areas like New York, London, and Tokyo. Though my salary remained the same, miraculously, "Lonely Voices" enabled us to increase our giving that year from $5.00 to $55.00 per week!

In one instance through music, He taught us to thank Him for a "no." In the other we have been privileged to thank Him for almost twenty years for a "yes."

The adventure of living by faith is the gateway to a life of thanksgiving! Faith doesn't beg or plead; it patiently listens and then obediently responds to the inner prompting of the Holy Spirit's leadership. As Christians have always emphasized, faith says, "Thank you." When God makes a promise faith believes it, accepts it, and moves ahead in gratitude. We are to "Enter His gates with thanksgiving. . . ."[21]

10
Intercession

Years ago while I was ministering in another country, a very concerned woman and her daughter waited outside the church building to talk with me at the close of a service. The mother explained that her husband, a prominent businessman in the area, was a hardened agnostic. He felt no need in his life for God and basically worshipped his possessions and his good health. I assured them that I would join them in the prayer that God would bring him to see his need for the Savior. As we talked, I recalled the verse which says, ". . . if two of you agree on earth about anything that they may ask, it shall be done for them by My Father who is in heaven." [1]

Unexpectedly, the lady's husband arrived in his new black Cadillac, a rarity in that part of the world, where American cars were extremely scarce. His erect bearing, expensive black leather jacket, and muscular build accented an egotistical spirit.

His wife introduced us but made a classic mistake by saying something like, "Honey, I have asked this gentleman to pray for you." I could almost see his mind working: "This man is a complete stranger. Why do I need *his* prayers? And furthermore, what do I need anyway?"

Though I hoped my face didn't show it, I wanted to find

the nearest rock and crawl under it! Quickly and silently I prayed, "Father, what do I do now? If he asks me to pray, what should I request?"

After an awkward silence, the man replied, "Sure. Everybody could use a little prayer now and then." Polite sarcasm tinged his response.

Almost instantly, my prayer for guidance was answered. The Holy Spirit reminded me to intercede for him by praying against his two most obvious areas of idolatry. If his money and good health were keeping him from seeing his need for Christ, they were his enemies rather than blessings. I was a little afraid when the Lord told me what to pray, because the prayer was unusual and specific, and because it could easily be misunderstood.

For these reasons, I looked directly into his eyes and very slowly and purposely said, "Sir, I do not believe you want me to pray for you, because God has already told me what to pray for, and I don't think you are going to like it."

With a little less sarcasm, he replied, "No, I want you to pray for me."

I warned him again that he would not like what I was going to request. I further explained that he could be sure the prayer would be answered because the Lord had specifically told me what to ask for.

As we talked, the expressions on the faces of his wife and daughter indicated how earnestly they expected God to guide our conversation and to convict him of his need. Encouraged, I said, "All right. Let's pray." He answered, "You mean, right now?" I said, "Yes, if we're going to do it, let's do it now."

We bowed our heads, and I felt that deep assurance and authority that God provides at such moments. "Father," I prayed, "in the name of Your Son Jesus Christ, in order that this man might know that there is a God in heaven who is real and who answers prayer, and that he might come to realize his need of the Savior, please let him go bankrupt six months from today and be flat on his back in the hospital when that occurs. When these things come to pass, please let him understand that they are for his good and a sign that You love him. Amen."

As we opened our eyes and raised our heads, he sarcastically said, "Thanks!" But almost simultaneously a joyful affirmation and "Amen" came from the lips of his wife and daughter. I can scarcely remember greater evidence of selfless love! They were willing to lose everything in order that he might be convicted of his sin.

About eight weeks later, a thrilling letter arrived at our home in Texas. The man's teenage daughter recounted the events of the two-month period. Her father was plagued by sleepless nights. How would he pay his hospital bills when he was bankrupt? And how could he earn money while sick in bed? Feverishly, he attempted to hide money to pay for his coming medical expenses. God had gotten his full attention!

He was experiencing what the Bible calls conviction of sin. Such treatment may seem harsh and such a prayer unloving, until one stops to realize that God isn't broke and both funds and good health can easily be restored if and when He feels it is in our best interest.

The girl's letter was literally an epistle of *joy* as she described her father's conversion and acceptance of Christ. After years of indifference, he had been jolted into attending a nearby church eight times in two months. On the eighth visit, he finally admitted his need, abandoned his defenses, and committed his life to the Savior.

At this point, people typically ask, "What happened four months later? Did God take away his money and his health?" He would have, exactly on schedule, but the man gave his resources and his health to God on the night that he became a Christian.

When our idolatry ceases and we begin to seek the kingdom of God, the very things which were enemies to our heavenly Father become tools for good in His hands. Let me illustrate.

Years later as I related this experience during a Bible conference in another country, a missionary stood to his feet in the middle of the service. He said, "May I finish your story?" and proceeded to tell us what had happened to that same man in subsequent years.

He reported how the man had grown spiritually and become a widely known, respected Christian leader in his country. He frequently used his black Cadillac to assist the Prime Minister by picking up visiting dignitaries at the airport. While driving them to their destination, he would share his testimony and express his gratitude and love for Christ. The very symbol of his alienation from God became a means of serving Him.

Praying for the Lost

The previous story illustrates praying for conviction of sin. This is the easiest kind of intercession and is probably the best place to start. You can intercede for others with great boldness and confidence when you ask the Holy Spirit to convict lost people who are unbelieving and saved people who are living in spiritual compromise. When explaining the basis for this powerful kind of prayer, Jesus once said that when the Holy Spirit comes He will *"convict* the world concerning sin." [2]

The whole point of intercessory prayer is asking God *to do what He already desires to accomplish.* Conviction of sin is clearly His will, and He will always honor our prayers when we make that request. Pause to consider the implications. Imagine what could happen if we began to ask for conviction of sin in the lives of those around us.

God is patiently waiting for us to pray for conviction. He is waiting for us to agree with Him about the light and the spiritual help He wants to bring into the lives of those in darkness. Jesus was called the "light of the world," but the Scriptures say that "men loved the darkness rather than the light; for their deeds were evil . . . everyone who does evil hates the light, and does not come to the light, lest his deeds should be exposed. But he who practices the truth comes to the light that his deeds may be manifested as having been wrought in God." [3] The result of our intercession is that God illuminates the hearts of those for whom we pray so they can see and forsake whatever keeps them in spiritual darkness.

Although some prayers are answered immediately, intercession often requires patience. Consider a puzzle. Individual pieces have to wait until the pattern begins to form. Only when finished can we see the whole. God alone can see each event which must come to pass in order for Him to bless us as He answers our prayers.

As God's children, we are given glimpses of His great plans, but even then *patience* is required. We must remember that "with the Lord one day is as a thousand years, and a thousand years as one day." [4] Our concept of time has little significance to God. What matters to Him is faith, truth, love, and character. These aspects of life have lasting value, but they are developed slowly. When you pray, you must be careful to "let patience have its perfect work, that you may be perfect and complete, lacking nothing." [5]

Praying for the Sick

Another form of intercession deals with praying for physical health. James says, "Is anyone among you sick? Let him call for the elders of the church, and let them pray over him, anointing him with oil in the name of the Lord." [6]

This kind of intercession is in some ways more difficult to practice than praying for the lost. The Scriptures make it clear that God "is patient . . . not wishing for any to perish but for all to come to repentance." [7] His will is not so obvious with regard to physical health. He *always* wants the spiritually sick to be healed, but it is **not** always His purpose for the physically sick to be healed. When praying for someone to be convicted of sin, you know God's will in advance, but when you pray for someone who is sick this is not the case. There are those whom God wills to heal, and those whom He does not.

When Healing Is God's Will

To pray effectively for someone who is sick, first analyze your own spiritual condition. Does your prayer come from a *clean* heart? The Scripture says, "Confess your sins to one another, and pray for one another, so that you may be healed." [8] Is your prayer offered in the calm assurance that God is able to answer it? The Scripture says, "The prayer offered in faith will restore the one who is sick." [9] This is the kind of intercession that is experienced when the conditions of *personal purity* and *faith* are present in the lives of those who are making the request and it is specifically the Father's will to restore the person's health. On such occasions we are privileged to offer what James calls "effective prayer"—the kind that comes when a righteous man seeks God's will in faith. This is the intercession that accomplishes much. [10]

A mature understanding of this teaching should lead every Christian to take continual inventory of his walk with God. Why? Because if things are not morally, ethically, and spiritually right in your life, the effectiveness of your prayers will be hindered and you will be powerless. Let's assume, however, that you have both purity and faith, but your intercession for the healing of a friend or loved one is still answered with a "no." This leads us to the second category of intercession for healing.

When Healing Is Not God's Will

Several years ago, as a guest speaker at a college in California, I met an unforgettable young man. Jerry is a quadriplegic. He has little stumps for arms, and one foot attached to the middle of his torso. He travels in a motorized wheelchair.

A close friend, who is a professor on that campus, told me about the ministry Jerry carries out on the college parking lot. He loves kids and stacks them on his wheelchair, driving it about as they scream with delight. He allows no one to feel sorry for him and is obviously happier than many of the physically healthy people on campus who are handicapped in other ways.

His roving wheelchair is unmistakable, because it displays bumper stickers like "God Loves You," and "Praise the Lord!" Popularly known as a person who is excited about Christ, Jerry ministers in a unique fashion by wearing a bootie on his foot which he calls a "Wordless Book." Each toe is knit in a different color. As he points at the gold toe, he explains its meaning: "God is the ruler of heaven, and He wants you to know Him and experience His love." The next toe is dark, so he explains the problem of sin.

Curiously the neighborhood children ask about the red toe, and he tells them how Christ shed His blood for their sins. Pointing to the white toe, he continues: "That's what Christ wants to do in your life: He desires to enter your heart and make you clean by forgiving your sins." By the last toe, which is green, they are spellbound as he tells them how God wants them to grow spiritually and become productive in the lives of others. Kids eat it up!

My friend and I do not know if God has led faithful Christians to ask that He heal Jerry and provide his missing limbs. We do know, however, that God is totally aware of Jerry's circumstances. It is also safe to assume that people of faith know Jerry, care about his condition, and would *eagerly* join in asking for such a miracle if God ever prompted them to do so.

If this is true, why would God allow Jerry to be left with the body of a quadriplegic? The very fact that he is a quadriplegic sets him apart and gives him the platform from which he bears his powerful witness for Christ.

Jerry demonstrates his faith on a daily basis; therefore, his physical condition does not indicate a lack of faith on his part, nor is it a reflection upon the faith of others. Once this is understood, our thoughts immediately turn from *pity* to *privilege.* What a compliment it is to Jerry that God would see within him the strength and character needed to carry out the sacred and challenging task to which he has been called. Jerry reminds me of the apostle Paul who, though pure and strong in faith, lived with a physical infirmity which made him more usable for God's glory.

Physical illness needs to be positively understood. Although the Lord raised Lazarus from the dead, later He also allowed him to die a second time. The Scriptures do not tell us how he died, but we assume that an illness was probably responsible. The same is true of every other person whom Christ healed or brought back to life during His earthly ministry.

Why did God allow them to die again? Because since the time of Adam, His plan has been to share heaven with those who have believed in Him and placed their faith in His Son. Jesus said, "Let not your heart be troubled; believe in God, believe also in Me. In My Father's house are many dwelling places; if it were not so, I would have told you; for I go to prepare a place for you. And if I go and prepare a place for you, I will come again, and receive you to Myself; that where I am, there you may be also." [11]

Do not for one moment think that Lazarus, who had already experienced heaven for four days, yearned to return and continue living here on earth. His attitude was probably more like that of the apostle Paul, who said, "I am hard-pressed from both directions, having the desire to depart and be with Christ, for that is very much better; yet to remain on in the flesh is more necessary for your sake." [12]

The only reasons Lazarus, Paul, or any other Christian would want to stay on earth would be for the sake of ministry and for fellowship with those family members and people whom they love. Beyond that, the new body we will receive, the glorious union with Christ, the fellowship with the departed saints who have gone before us, and the joys of heaven itself make death the closest friend of every believer. Without death, we could not shed the frailties of this life or receive the wonders that await us in the kingdom Christ has prepared on our behalf.

Because accidents account for the deaths of only a few, it is sickness which God most often uses to fulfill His will in our lives and bring us into the kingdom of heaven. Those who fear death need to be reminded that the grave has lost its victory and death has lost its sting.[13] There is nothing to be feared in going to sleep and waking up in the presence of the Savior.

If it were not for death, the billions who have lived in the world's history would have overpopulated the earth and turned it into a hellish existence with no escape. Christ has taken man's worst enemy and used it for a higher purpose.

Intercession must never be thought of as trying to persuade God to do something He really does not want to do. It is not an effort to corner Him in a theological box where certain verses are used to make Him perform according to our will, rather than His. Your objective is to *agree* with him and to claim those things which please Him, even though they may cut straight across the grain of your human nature. Of course you hate to lose a loved one or to see a young man handicapped like Jerry, but be careful to listen as you pray. If God speaks to you as He did to Paul and the answer is "no," by faith be prepared to praise Him as much as if the answer were "yes." You can afford to do this, because He knows what is best for you and no request which you bring to Him as His child will ever go unheard or unanswered.

Jesus, the Intercessor

As you read your Bible, you will soon become aware that the Lord Jesus lived a life of intercession. His petitions were always directed toward the needs of those He loved. He never asked for a palace, a chariot or an extensive wardrobe for Himself, as is evidenced by the fact that He didn't have them. He came into the world to seek and save the lost,[14] and He left the world to prepare a heavenly home for those same people. His whole life was spent seeking benefit for others. He lived and breathed intercession. Even on the cross He interceded for sinners of all the ages when He uttered this prayer in pain: "Father, forgive them; for they do not know what they are doing." [15]

We are given a glimpse into Jesus' early ministry of intercession when, speaking to the twelve, He turned His attention to Simon Peter, saying, "Simon, Simon, Satan has asked to sift you as wheat. But I have prayed for you . . . that your faith may not fail. And when you have returned to me, strengthen your brothers." [16]

It was Christ's prayer that restored Peter to useful service after his darkest hour. It was intercession that helped Peter come to true repentance after he had denied the Lord Jesus Christ three times. In his own testimony, written many years later, he said, "The Lord knows how to rescue the godly from temptation." [17] Paul brings this into focus for us today when he declares, "No temptation has overtaken you but such as is common to man; and God is faithful, who will not allow you to be tempted beyond what you are able, but with the temptation will provide the way of escape also, that you may be able to endure it." [18]

Jesus' longest and best-known personal prayer is found in the seventeenth chapter of John. Lifting His eyes toward heaven, His prayer was characterized by words like these: "I ask on their behalf" [19]; and "I do not ask in behalf of these alone, but for those also who (will) believe in Me. . . ." [20]

He continued by beseeching the Father not to take us out of this world but to keep us away from the influence of Satan. His prayer was consistent with His emphasis that Christians should live *in* the world but not be *like* it.[21]

Jesus' intercession for the disciples intensified as He came toward the close of His earthly ministry. He was leaving His devoted followers behind, and He knew they would face trials and temptations with the potential of overwhelming their faith. To prepare them for the hard times to come, He told them about the future: "They will put you out of the synagogue; in fact, a time is coming when anyone who kills you will think he is offering a service to God." [22]

In His deep concern that they not feel deserted during His time of persecution, He told them of a Helper He would send to be with them in the near future.[23] He promised that this Helper would bear witness to His divinity,[24] recall His teachings to their remembrance,[25] guide them,[26] disclose the future to them,[27] explain the truths of God,[28] and convict the world concerning sin, righteousness and judgment.[29] As the result of His intercession [30] this Helper, the Holy Spirit, would come to indwell and empower them to be His witnesses beginning in Jerusalem and finally to the remotest parts of the earth.[31]

After the Lord ascended to heaven, His ministry of intercession continued. He simply changed His location! Upon His departure, "Christ did not enter a holy place made with hands, a mere copy of the true one, but into heaven itself, now to appear in the presence of God for us." [32] The writer of Hebrews goes on to explain that Christ "always lives to make intercession" [33] for us and ". . . is able to save forever those who draw near to God *through Him.*" [34]

Without Christ interceding for us, there would be no hope for the human race. Why is this true? Isaiah expressed it in these dramatic words: "All our righteousness is as filthy rags" [35] and stench in the nostrils of a holy God. Paul said, "There is none righteous, no, not one." [36] Without Christ's many prayers on our behalf and His selfless act of intercession when He took our place on the cross, we would be doomed to the penalty we deserve because of our sin. How eternally grateful we can be that Christ cared enough to pray and give Himself on our behalf. He was the perfect intercessor!

Interceding for others is the most *Christlike, unselfish* praying that you and I will ever do. It includes praying for the lost and praying for the saved, praying for the sick and praying for the well. It reaches out in faith and affects the lives of people next door and in the remotest part of the world. It is urgent, yet patient. And above all else, it seeks the will of God in every situation.

11
Learning to Listen to God

Be still, and know that I am God. (Psalm 46:10a, KJV)

The pinnacle of spiritual growth is a godly character, and the queen of the disciplines that produce that character is meditation. Over the centuries, the number of Christians who have really understood and practiced this art have been few.

Biblically, those who have given the world its clearest understanding of divine truth have been its greatest meditators. In addition to the Lord Himself, these include biblical leaders such as John, who authored a Gospel, several Epistles and the Book of Revelation; Paul, who expressed Hebrew faith in a way that could be understood by Gentiles; David, who taught us how to worship through his Psalms; Solomon, who confounded the ancients with his wisdom; and Daniel, whose commitment to prayer won the respect of pagan kings.

In today's busy world there is a pronounced resurgence of interest in the timeless value of meditation. Unfortunately, however, the Far Eastern concept of meditation is more popularly known than the scriptural emphasis upon fellowship with the Living God. It was God's Word, not the "nothingness" of transcendental meditation, that was the object of the psalmist's meditation day and night.[1]

For each truth there seems to be a counterfeit, but Christian meditation is far too valuable to be confused with fads and empty introspection. However severe the excesses may be, properly understood it is unquestionably the friend of spiritual growth.

Receiving the highest benefit from hearing God's Word in church, Bible reading, or study, will come about through quietly meditating on what has been taught. The same holds true for Scripture Memory. The psalmist said, "I will *meditate* on Thy precepts, and . . . *delight* in Thy statutes; I shall not *forget Thy word.*"[2]

Clearly, Moses understood this same concept. He said, "And these words, which I am commanding you today, shall be on your heart; and you shall teach them diligently to your sons and shall talk of them when you sit in your house and when you walk by the way and when you lie down and when you rise up."[3] Whether you hear or read God's Word, it will reside in your heart through the practice of thinking about it over and over again.

The Secret of Pondering

Mary, the mother of Jesus, is the foremost example of this spiritual discipline. Her meditation stands out as a model for us today. In Luke the angel Gabriel spoke to Mary, saying, " 'Hail, favored one! The Lord is with you.' But she was greatly troubled at this statement, and *kept pondering* what kind of salutation this might be."[4] Pondering means to think about something repeatedly. When the Scripture says that Mary kept thinking about Gabriel's words, we are not to assume she did it in the few minutes while he was speaking.

Other verses indicate that as the years went by, she meditated on his words again and again. "What did he mean . . . that I was a favored person and the Lord was with me?" She understood intellectually what she heard in her own Aramaic language, but pondering is deeper. Pondering is a different quality of thought. "What did he mean? And how will it affect my life?"

Gabriel went on to say, "He will be great (speaking of Jesus), and will be called the Son of the Most High; and the Lord God will give Him the throne of His father David; and He will reign over the house of Jacob forever; and His kingdom will have no end." [5]

What if you had been Mary and an angel had said that to you? Over the years, I believe you would have given that message the benefit of your deepest contemplation. Why should we spend less time pondering His words when we read or hear them today? Are they not just as surely His words to us?

Note Mary's reaction: "And Mary said, 'Behold, the bondslave of the Lord; be it done to me according to your word.' And the angel departed from her." [6] How do you like her response? When Sarah, Abraham's wife, was spoken to by an angel, she laughed.[7] But Mary received Gabriel's words, took them as from God, in faith, and immediately began to meditate on their meaning.

The second angelic announcement about Jesus' birth came to Joseph in a dream. The angel said to him that the child within Mary had been conceived of the Holy Spirit and would be a boy whom Joseph should name Jesus, because He would save His people from their sins.[8]

A few months later, on the night when Joseph and Mary arrived in Bethlehem for the census under Caesar Augustus,[9] a great miracle took place. While shepherds were in the fields watching their flocks, an angel of the Lord stood before them.[10] The beautiful glory that had been seen several times in the Old Testament enveloped the shepherds—and the angel had their undivided attention! They were terribly frightened. The angel said to them, "Do not be afraid; for behold, I bring you good news of a great joy which shall be for all the people; for today in the city of David there has been born for you a Savior, who is Christ the Lord." [11]

Based on the first angelic message that "His kingdom will have no end," Mary might have thought that Jesus would be like other earthly kings—with the understanding that He would literally have descendants on the throne of David forever. But the second visitation provided a much deeper understanding. This king would actually be able to save people from the power of sin. This had never been said about any king before.

The third announcement, which was made to the shepherds, far overshadowed the others. These words are undoubtedly among the most significant in the history of the world: "Today in the city of David there has been born for you a Savior, who is *Christ the Lord.*" [12] The actual word which the angel used—*Messiah*—was well-known to every devout Jew before, during, and after this historic event. The Greek word for Messiah, which has become so familiar to people of every nation, is the word "Christ." Jesus, which literally means Savior, was the Lord's earthly name. Messiah, or Christ, was not His last name, but rather the divine title reserved for Him and given to Him by His Heavenly Father.

The Dawning of Understanding

Many years later, when the aged apostle Peter wrote his second letter, he reflected on the unforgettable occasion when God indelibly impressed Jesus' true identity upon his heart: "For we did not follow cleverly devised tales when we made known to you the power and coming of our Lord Jesus Christ, but we were eyewitnesses of His majesty. For when He received honor and glory from God the Father, such an utterance as this was made to Him, . . . 'This is My beloved Son with whom I am well pleased,'—and we ourselves heard this utterance made from heaven when we were with Him on the holy mountain." [13]

It took time for Mary and those who had the privilege of personally knowing the Messiah in His humanity to understand the unfathomable dimensions of His kingdom. It was so much more than even the most devout Jewish believers and prophets had dared to dream or hope for.

Peter refers to this fact, saying, "This salvation was something the prophets did not fully understand. Though they wrote about it, they had many questions as to what it all could mean. They wondered what the Spirit of Christ within them was talking about, for he told them to write down the events which, since then, have happened to Christ: his suffering, and his great glory afterwards. And they wondered when and to whom all this would happen. They were finally told that these things would not occur during their lifetime . . . now at last this Good News has been plainly announced to all of us. It was preached to us in the power of the same heaven-sent Holy Spirit who spoke to them;

and it is all so strange and wonderful that even the angels in heaven would give a great deal to know more about it." [14]

When Peter wrote these words, he undoubtedly thought back to the time when Jesus spoke to him and the other apostles saying, "To you it has been granted to know the mysteries of the kingdom of heaven . . . blessed are your eyes, because they see and your ears because they hear. For truly I say to you, that many prophets and righteous men desired to see what you see and did not see it; and to hear what you hear, and did not hear it." [15]

In one sense, Mary and Joseph were like the early Hebrew prophets who had to walk by faith as understanding gradually dawned in their hearts and minds. On that majestic night, when the solitary angel was joined by the heavenly multitude, the shepherds said: " 'Let us go straight to Bethlehem then, and see this thing that has happened which the Lord has made known to us.' And they came in haste and found their way to Mary and Joseph, and the baby as He lay in the manger." [16] And "when the shepherds saw him, they told them what the angel had said about the child. All who heard it were amazed at what the shepherds said." [17] "But Mary treasured up all these things, pondering them in her heart." [18]

Mary had already been meditating for nine months, wondering, "What does it mean that I have been overshadowed by the power of the Most High, and my holy offspring shall be called the Son of God?" Suddenly, with the announcement of the shepherds, she and Joseph were told His identity in words of unmistakable significance—He is the Messiah!

If that were not enough, eight days later, when the infant Jesus was taken to Jerusalem to be dedicated to the Lord, His identity was confirmed again. A godly man named Simeon who had been assured ". . . that he would not die before he had seen the Lord's promised Messiah . . . took the child in his arms and gave thanks to God, saying: 'Now, Lord, you have kept your promise, and you may let your servant go in peace. With my own eyes I have seen your salvation' . . ." [19] Next, another stranger, whose name was Anna, ". . . came along just as Simeon was talking with Mary and Joseph, and she also began thanking God and telling everyone in Jerusalem who had been awaiting the coming of the Savior that the Messiah had finally arrived." [20]

The miracle of His virgin birth and the repeated testimony of men, women, and angels were on Mary's mind. By the time Jesus had reached the age of twelve, it was clear that He also knew His identity. When Joseph and Mary visited Jerusalem to observe a religious holy day called the Passover, Jesus could not be found for three days. Needless to say, His parents were greatly concerned until they discovered Him sitting among the Hebrew teachers. The Scripture says, "And all who heard Him were amazed at His understanding and His answers." [21]

Joseph's and Mary's spontaneous response upon finding Him there was one of astonishment rather than anger. Jesus' question, which seemed so obvious to Him, was still a puzzle to them when He asked, "Why is it that you were looking for Me? Did you not know that I had to be in My Father's house?" [22] Jesus understood who He was, but the Scripture says, "They did not understand the statement which He had made to them. And He went down with them, and came to Nazareth; and He continued in subjection to them; and His mother *treasured* all these things in her heart." [23]

On every step of the journey, Mary's response was one of meditation. For thirty years she lived with a perfect Son. It is impossible to put ourselves in her place. No one before and no one since has ever reared a sinless son. In all likelihood, it was Mary's willingness to meditate upon what God had said which qualified her for the high privilege of providing human love and an earthly home for the Savior.

From childhood Jesus knew that His father was—The Father. We know little about the details of His life from the age of twelve to thirty. However, the words and events surrounding these brief years sank deeply into Mary's heart. Undoubtedly there were mixed emotions. Certainly there were questions. When would He do something? She learned the virtues of faith and patience while waiting for Him to move away from carpentry into the divine mission for which He had been sent.

Finally, at a wedding in Cana of Galilee, Mary was obviously aware of His ability to help in a potentially embarrassing situation.[24] There, at the age of thirty, He performed the first miraculous sign which pointed to His identity. It was only a beginning, but at last her expectations and hopes were beginning to come true.

A New Generation

God is looking for a generation of Christians who will take His Word seriously and spend as much time *listening* as they do *speaking* in prayer. *Listening* is the side of prayer from which wisdom, guidance, and understanding come. When the Lord discovers that you, like Mary, are willing to meditate and then follow through in obedience, He will be able to trust you with increased responsibility and the privilege of service.

About mid-way through college, I realized that God wasn't doing much in my life, and I wondered why. Though I loved Him, the sense of warmth was lacking in our relationship. God seemed to be using my friends, but for some reason He was not using me.

After several miserable weeks, I went out to a quiet place to pout! That afternoon, an elderly minister came to talk with me. I told him, among other things, that God had been calling my attention to a portion of Jesus' Sermon on the Mount each time I read the Bible: "Do not give what is holy to dogs, and do not throw your pearls before swine." [25] As we looked at the verse together he asked, "Billie, what have you done with the spiritual insights God has already given you?"

I had been a Christian for only a few years, and I had not yet learned how to treat spiritual pearls. When the Lord gave me an insight from a sermon, I never wrote it down. The same was true of lessons from my Bible study. It was impossible for me to meditate on the insights I received, because I forgot them almost as soon as I heard them.

Meditation requires enough dedication on our part to ensure that we make careful note of what God tells us. Like so many new believers, I was running on sincere enthusiasm without the benefit of personal discipline.

Through the helpful time spent with this wise counselor, I saw that my lack of knowledge and discipline had been making me act like the dog or the swine in Jesus' illustration. A dog does not know how to appreciate something valuable—if you give the best dog in the world a new Bible, he will simply bury it or chew it up. And a pig has less than zero ability to appreciate a pearl!

Part of maturing is learning that scriptural insights are to be polished with meditation. Repeatedly, Jesus said, "He who has ears to hear, let him hear!" [26] This was an invitation to meditate upon the truth of His words.

When Jesus delivered a boy from bondage to an unclean spirit, He rebuked His disciples for failing to help the child due to their unbelief. He asked, "How long shall I be with you?" [27] Then He said, "Let these words *sink into your ears;* for the Son of Man is going to be delivered into the hands of men." [28] He wanted His disciples to think deeply. They needed to let His words settle and lodge in their hearts. He was leaving, and the ministry which had been His would soon be theirs. Would they be ready?

The same searching question must be asked in your life today. Are you ready to pick up the baton of ministry which has been handed from one generation to the other by the Lord's disciples? Are you willing to fulfill your destiny?

Inner peace and joy are the result of God-ordained service. And that service is the result of spiritual growth. In this process the cycle of love is made complete—and the journey never ends!

Your Christian life started through believing in Christ and loving Him as your Lord and Savior. Now you are on the journey of **joyful** obedience and spiritual growth. The disciplines you have learned are not ends in themselves. They are merely ways of nurturing the love you hold in your heart for your Lord who said, **"If you love me, keep My commandments."** [29]

End Notes

Chapter 1

1. Luke 23:42, NKJV
2. Psalm 37:4–5
3. Luke 15:11–32

Chapter 2

1. Matthew 10:32, NIV
2. 1 Corinthians 9:24, 2 Timothy 4:7
3. Romans 10:17, JB
4. Matthew 4:4, NKJV
5. Nehemiah 8:2–6, Paraphrased
6. Animists are those who still hold ancient pagan beliefs about multiple gods and spirits, usually active in nature.
7. Psalm 32:8

Chapter 3

1. Mark 1:21–34
2. John 14:10
3. Mark 1:27
4. Mark 1:36–37
5. John 3:34
6. Colossians 2:9

7. Matthew 8:23–27
8. Psalm 127:2b, NKJV
9. 1 Timothy 4:7
10. Psalm 46:10a, KJV
11. Psalm 119:103
12. Jeremiah 15:16
13. 1 Corinthians 1:9, Phillips

Chapter 4

1. 1 Timothy 4:7b
2. 1 Corinthians 2:14
3. KJV
4. Philippians 3:7–8a
5. Colossians 3:1a, 2
6. "For God so loved the world, that he gave his only begotten Son, that whosoever believeth in him should not perish, but have everlasting life." (KJV)
7. Phillips
8. Phillipians 3:10a, KJV
9. Psalm 90:14, Paraphrased
10. Exodus 12:37
11. KJV
12. 1 Samuel 13:14
13. 2 Samuel 11
14. Psalm 32:8
15. Galatians 6:9, LB
16. Romans 8:1
17. Hebrews 12:6, Paraphrased
18. Romans 8:37b, NIV
19. Philippians 3:14, KJV

Chapter 5

1. James 1:4
2. Matthew 6:9–13
3. John 6:35
4. Matthew 4:4b, NIV
5. KJV
6. Luke 14:26, Paraphrased
7. Matthew 22:37, NIV
8. John 13:34
9. KJV
10. Proverbs 23:7a, NKJV
11. Proverbs 4:23, KJV
12. 1 John 2:15b, KJV
13. Mark 12:29–30
14. Matthew 17:1

15. Revelation 19:6
16. Luke 12:34, KJV
17. 1 Chronicles 29:9
18. Psalm 24:1
19. Matthew 28:19–20, 24:14
20. 2 Corinthians 5:21
21. 1 Corinthians 6:19
22. 1 Corinthians 6:20
23. John 3:16
24. Luke 5:15–16
25. Mark 6:34, NIV
26. Mark 6:45–46
27. Mark 6:47–48
28. Luke 6:12
29. Mark 14:32–36, NIV
30. James 1:5
31. James 4:2b, KJV
32. Matthew 7:12, LB
33. Mark 10:45, Paraphrased
34. Matthew 10:24
35. John 4:4–26
36. John 3:1–15
37. Zacchaeus—Luke 19
    Lazarus—John 11
    Joseph—Matthew 27:57
    Paul (Saul)—Acts 8
    Peter—Matthew 4:18
    John Mark—Acts 13:13
    Mary Magdalene—Luke 8:2
    Mary of Bethany—John 11
38. Romans 8:5a, TEV
39. John 10:10, KJV
40. Philippians 2:13, KJV

Chapter 6

1. Psalm 31:19a
2. Exodus 7–17; 24:15 ff; Deuteronomy 29:5
3. Deuteronomy 3:24
4. Psalm 8:1a
5. Revelation 4:11, KJV
6. Psalm 34:1
7. Matthew 3:17
8. Matthew 6:9–10
9. Colossians 1:15–17
10. Philippians 2:9–11
11. Romans 11:33–34
12. Hebrews 11:6

13. 1 Peter 1:8
14. 1 Peter 1:3

Chapter 7

1. Jeremiah 33:3
2. John 16:24
3. John 16:27
4. John 16:17b, 25
5. John 16:26
6. Acts 4:12
7. Hebrews 4:16a, KJV
8. Matthew 20:28b
9. 1 Peter 1:18–19, KJV
10. John 14:14, NKJV
11. James 4:2c, KJV
12. James 4:3a
13. Luke 11:1
14. John 14:26
15. John 14:13
16. John 15:7
17. John 3:3
18. Jeremiah 15:16, KJV
19. 1 John 5:14–15
20. ". . . not my will, but Thine be done." Luke 22:42b
21. Psalm 37:4
22. Psalm 19:14
23. 1 Chronicles 28:9b
24. Psalm 84:11b
25. James 4:3
26. Numbers 11:14, NIV
27. Numbers 11:15b
28. Numbers 11:17b, LB
29. Philippians 4:6, LB
30. Isaiah 41:10, NKJV
31. Luke 1:37
32. Luke 22:42, NIV
33. John 17:4, NKJV
34. 2 Corinthians 12:8–9
35. Galatians 4:13–15
36. Galatians 6:11
37. ". . . but Trophimus I left sick at Miletus." 2 Timothy 4:20b
38. ". . . there was given me a thorn in the flesh, a messenger of Satan to buffet me—to keep me from exalting myself!" 2 Corinthians 12:7b
39. 2 Corinthians 12:9
40. 2 Corinthians 12:10b
41. Acts 16:22–34
42. Romans 8:28, NKJV

43. 2 Corinthians 6:4–6
44. Exodus 33:13a, NKJV
45. Exodus 33:14
46. Philippians 4:6
47. Philippians 4:7, NKJV

Chapter 8

1. 1 John 1:9, KJV
2. Psalm 51:17b, LB
3. KJV
4. James 4:17, NIV
5. Malachi 3:8, 10, LB
6. John 14:15, NKJV
7. Proverbs 3:27, NIV
8. Romans 14:23b, KJV
9. 1 Samuel 10:8
10. Galatians 3:11, KJV
11. James 1:13–15
12. Romans 3:23, NKJV
13. Jeremiah 17:9a, KJV
14. Matthew 12:34b, NKJV
15. Matthew 15:19, LB
16. Psalm 51:10, KJV
17. Matthew 5:28, LB
18. Proverbs 4:23, NKJV
19. Matthew 3:8
20. John 8:11b, KJV
21. 2 Corinthians 6:14a, LB
22. 2 Corinthians 6:15b, LB
23. Philippians 4:19
24. 2 Corinthians 5:21
25. Romans 3:10, Paraphrased
26. Hebrews 7:26–27
27. Hebrews 4:15
28. Psalm 66:18, LB
29. James 5:16a
30. Matthew 5:23–24, NKJV
31. Philippians 4:13, NKJV

Chapter 9

1. Romans 8:28, NKJV
2. Hebrews 13:5b, NKJV
3. John 16:33b, NIV
4. Luke 2:10b–11a
5. Luke 17:11–16a, LB
6. Matthew 15:36

7. Matthew 26:27
8. James 1:17
9. Romans 1:20–21, LB
10. 1 Thessalonians 5:18
11. Acts 16:25, Paraphrased
12. Daniel 3:28
13. Ephesians 5:20
14. Matthew 25:21
15. Matthew 6:33, NKJV
16. Matthew 6:8b
17. Psalm 37:25
18. 1 Thessalonians 5:24
19. James 1:4, NKJV
20. Psalm 92:1
21. Psalm 100:4

Chapter 10

1. Matthew 18:19
2. John 16:8b
3. John 3:19b–21
4. 2 Peter 3:8b
5. James 1:4, NKJV
6. James 5:14
7. 2 Peter 3:9b
8. James 5:16a
9. James 5:15a
10. James 5:16b
11. John 14:1–3
12. Philippians 1:23–24
13. 1 Corinthians 15:55–57
14. Luke 19:10
15. Luke 23:34a
16. Luke 22:31, NIV
17. 2 Peter 2:9a
18. 1 Corinthians 10:13
19. John 17:9
20. John 17:20
21. John 17:15–16
22. John 16:2, NIV
23. John 15:26
24. John 16:14
25. John 14:26
26. John 16:13
27. John 16:14
28. John 16:15
29. John 16:8
30. Romans 8:26

31. Acts 1:8
32. Hebrews 9:24
33. Hebrews 7:25c
34. Hebrews 7:25a, b
35. Isaiah 64:6, paraphrased
36. Romans 3:10, KJV

Chapter 11

1. Psalm 1:2
2. Psalm 119:15a, 16
3. Deuteronomy 6:6–7
4. Luke 1:28–29
5. Luke 1:32–33
6. Luke 1:38
7. Genesis 18:12
8. Matthew 1:19–21
9. Luke 2:1–7
10. Luke 2:8–9
11. Luke 2:10–11
12. Luke 2:11
13. 2 Peter 1:16–18
14. 1 Peter 1:10–12, LB
15. Matthew 13:11a, 16, 17
16. Luke 2:15–16
17. Luke 2:17–18, TEV
18. Luke 2:19
19. Luke 2:26, 28–30, TEV
20. Luke 2:38, LB
21. Luke 2:47
22. Luke 2:49
23. Luke 2:50–51
24. John 2:3–5
25. Matthew 7:6a
26. Matthew 11:15, NKJV
27. Luke 9:41
28. Luke 9:44
29. John 14:15

SPIRITUAL JOURNAL
by
Dr. Billie Hanks, Jr.
with
Billy Beacham

CONTENTS

I. QUIET TIME SECTION

How to use
Sample page
Scripture memory
Five aspects of prayer

Pages to fill in
Intercession
Scriptural insights and prayer (Weeks 1-4)

II NOTE TAKING SECTION

How to use
Sample page

Pages to fill in
Note taking

III ADDITIONAL AIDS

Pages to fill in
Church friends list
Quiet time highlights
Ministry goals and activities

HOW TO USE THE QUIET TIME SECTION

"Be still and know that I am God . . ." (Psalm 46:10a, KJV)

This page gives a simple outline for spending a quarter of an hour with God each day. It can be expanded on as you wish.

1. BEGIN YOUR 15-MINUTE QUIET TIME WITH PRAYER (30 seconds)

   This should be a *brief prayer* for understanding as you prepare to read God's Word.

2. PAUSE FOR MEDITATION (30 seconds)

   Meditate on the meaning of your selected memory verse for the week. Repeat it *out loud* several times, emphasizing the key words which make it meaningful. Seek to find verses that apply to your own spiritual growth. (There is space at the top of each Quiet Time page for your new memory verse.)

3. READ THE SCRIPTURES (5 minutes)

   You may choose to use the Bible Reading Plan included in your **Journal** (P.202); however, the Quiet Time Section will also work in conjunction with *any other* plan you select. Regardless of the approach you are led to take, remember that consistency and expectancy are the secrets to spiritual growth in personal devotions.

4. RECORD INSIGHTS AND MAKE PERSONAL APPLICATION (3 minutes)

   Think about the meaning of what you read. NOTE: In the example on page 13, you will see several ways you can use symbols to identify and emphasize items which you wish to recall.

   To help make a personal application, you might ask these questions (they can be remembered by the acrostic SPACE):*

Is there a . . .	**Sin** for me to confess?
	Promise for me to claim?
	Attitude for me to change?
	Command for me to obey?
	Example for me to follow?

   *Used by permission, Rick Warren.

   WRITE OUT your thoughts and seek to make your applications PERSONAL, SPECIFIC and MEASURABLE.

5. SPEND TIME IN PRAYER (2 minutes)

   Ask God to guide you throughout the day and to provide opportunities for you to apply what you have learned during your Quiet Time. Instructions for five important aspects of prayer are on the following pages.

6. REVIEW MEMORY VERSES (4 minutes)

Review your verses from previous weeks, using the special *Review Section* at the top of your Quiet Time page.

END YOUR QUIET TIME, BUT CONTINUE THE DAY IN PRAYER.

SAMPLE PAGE – Scriptural Insights and Prayer

Scripture Memory Review	Date	Jan 7-13

Matt. 6:33
Josh. 1:8
Jer. 33:3
Psa. 46:10
Eph: 6:11

Memory Verse for the Week
1 Peter 1:15 *"But like the Holy One who called you, be holy yourselves also in all your behaviour."*

S	M	T	W	T	F	S
☑	☑	☑	☐	☐	☐	☐

Scriptural Insight	Prayer

SUNDAY

1 Peter 1:13 *"Gird your minds for action"* Don't just slide into the day. Meet it positively.

☆ vs. 14 *"former lusts"* Don't fall into the same old sin traps.

m vs. 15 Holiness is our objective.

x 1 Thess. 4:7 *". . . live a holy life."*

P Father, help my mind to stay centred on You today.

C Forgive me for thinking impure thoughts yesterday. Please continue to purify my mind.

Application:
I will prepare my mind for Christ-centred thoughts today by meditating on my Quiet Time insights while driving to work rather than listening to the radio.

MONDAY

➤ 1 Peter 2:13 *"Submit . . . to every human institution"* We are to be law-abiding and submissive to those in authority.

☆ vs 21 *"Christ also suffered . . . leaving an example"* Suffering is evidently part of becoming like our Lord.

C Forgive me for consistently breaking the speed limits.

T Lord, thank You for reminding me that you are not unfamiliar with pain and can identify fully with the times when my body hurts.

Application:
As from today, I will begin driving within the speed limits. Since most of my speeding comes from running late, I will need to be better organised.

TUESDAY

☆ 1 Peter 3:15 *"always being ready to make a defence"* I must be prepared to witness on any occasion. This desire will flow out of Christ being Lord in my life.

P Lord, you are aware of my burden for Sam. The last time we talked I couldn't answer his questions. Please enable me to be prepared for the next opportunity.

Application:
Tonight I will do some reading which will help me answer Sam next time.

☆	my meditation for today	A	Adoration
➤	further study needed	C	Confession
x	cross reference	T	Thanksgiving
m	verse(s) to memorize	P	Petition

SCRIPTURE MEMORY

"Thy word have I hid in mine heart, that I might not sin against thee."
(Psalm 119:11, KJV)

Normally, references are more easily forgotten than verses. Your review system helps overcome this problem by including spaces for six abbreviated references. Rewrite your references each Sunday morning during your Quiet Time. Quote the references out loud *before* and *after* saying each verse as you review it.

A verse is not truly memorized until you *cannot forget it*. Merely learning a verse is not your spiritual objective – live with the verse until it saturates your mind and affects the way you think and act. Good review is the basis for good meditation, and spiritual meditation produces the kind of thinking that builds a godly life. (Philippians 4:8)

Scripture memory requires consistency. Hold yourself accountable by checking the boxes provided by each reference. By simply reviewing each verse for six weeks, you will make a major step toward committing it to memory

Remember the admonition of Philippians 4:13: *"I can do all things through Christ which strengtheneth me." (KJV)* This includes hiding God's Word in your heart!

In this illustration you have already memorized five verses and said them out loud three times during the week.

You are now learning Philippians 4:13.

SAMPLE

Scripture Memory Review						Date	Jan. 7-13
Matt. 6:33							
Josh. 1:8						Memory Verse for the Week	
Jer. 33:3						Philippians 4:13 *"I can do all things through Christ*	
Psa. 46:10						*which strengtheneth me."*	
Eph. 6:11							
S	M	T	W	T	F	S	
☑	☑	☑	☐	☐	☐	☐	

FIVE ASPECTS OF PRAYER

1 ADORATION

(Praising God for Who He is)

"I will bless the Lord at all times; His praise shall continually be in my mouth." (Psalm 34:1, NAS)

There is no better way to *begin* a time of prayer than by expressing praise to God! Praise is the most important element of prayer, and it is probably one of the most neglected. In a prayer of adoration, you express your deep feelings toward God in response to His love, wisdom, presence, power, knowledge, grace, holiness, greatness and His other divine attributes. This kind of prayer will always be an occasion for joy!

As you enrol in the school of prayer, remember this important lesson: Our *adoration* must be reserved for God, not for projects, ministries or works done in His name. When you are in His will, the desire to praise Him will come naturally.

PRAISING GOD IN ADORATION

To help you experience this valuable form of prayer, several choice passages have been listed below.

MAJESTY – 1 Chron. 29:11, Psa. 8:9, Job 37:22

HOLINESS – Ex. 15:11, Isa. 6:3, 1 Pet. 1:14-16

The symbol "A" for "Adoration" is used in the code provided in the daily Quiet Time prayer section. As you read, you will find many verses which describe God's divine attributes. Make them the subject of your prayer.

S A M P L E	Scriptural Insight	Prayer
	➤ 1 Chron. 29:1-2 Although the temple bore Solomon's name, David actually provided the wealth of materials needed for its construction.	A Father, I join David this morning in saying that you are the very essence of greatness, power, glory, and victory. Everything everywhere belongs to You – including me.
	☆ v. 3 & 9 David gave with joy! v. 11 In his prayer of adoration he praised God for his greatness.	

Application: I will meditate throughout the day upon who God really is, and I will tell Him how proud I am to be His child.

☆	my meditation for today	A	Adoration
➤	further study needed	C	Confession
x	cross reference	T	Thanksgiving
m	verse(s) to memorize	P	Petition

2 CONFESSION
(Agreeing with God about your Sin)

"If we confess our sins, He is faithful and righteous to forgive us our sins and to cleanse us from all unrighteousness." (1 John 1:9, NAS)

Receiving God's gift of forgiveness is part of the miracle that occurs in a person's life when he accepts Christ as his Saviour. Choosing to accept this gift, made possible through the cross, establishes one's eternal *relationship* with God; however, it is our prayer life and obedience that maintain our *fellowship* with Him on a day-to-day basis.

Jesus said, *"If you love Me, you will keep My commandments"* (John 14:15, NAS). When we make self-centred and sinful decisions, our relationship with God remains the same, but the quality of our fellowship is strained. It is *confession* that restores the privilege of that wonderful fellowship.

HOW TO PRACTISE CONFESSION

As you use the daily Quiet Time portion of your **Journal**, note the single "C", which stands for "confession". A sincere prayer of confession will normally demand that a practical application be made.

Both sin and righteousness are the result of personal decisions, so *confession* that is based upon *genuine repentance* will be proved by a *change* in your daily life. For this reason, your greatest spiritual victories will normally come as the result of this honest, cleansing kind of prayer.

Your confession and repentance need to be *specific*.

		Scriptural Insight		Prayer
S **A** **M** **P** **L** **E**		Eph. 5:15b-16 *"wise, making the most of your time . . ."* Wise people use their time well!	C	Lord, I have been wasting a lot of time watching T.V. lately. These are hours I could have spent in Bible reading, prayer or service. Please forgive my misplaced attention.
	☆	vs. 17:20 The secret of using my time well is being controlled by the Holy Spirit.		

Application:
I will reduce my T.V. viewing to five hours
per week.

☆	my meditation for today	A	Adoration
➔	further study needed	C	Confession
x	cross reference	T	Thanksgiving
m	verse(s) to memorize	P	Petition

3 THANKSGIVING

(Expressing gratitude to God for What He Has Done)

"In everything give thanks; for this is God's will for you in Christ Jesus." (1 Thessalonians 5:18, NAS)

The average Christian probably spends too *much* time *asking* and too *little* time *thanking*.

Paul's admonition to *"give thanks in everything"* reflects the maturity of his Christian life. He had been shipwrecked, beaten, hungry, severely criticized and imprisoned – yet he could honestly write those words. Why? Because his heart was filled with gratitude! He expressed it like this:

"But whatever things were gain to me, those things I have counted as loss for the sake of Christ. More than that, I count all things to be loss in the view of the surpassing value of knowing Christ Jesus my Lord . . ." (Philippians 3:7-8, NAS)

Prayer provides the opportunity to express our deepest emotions and feelings to God. How long has it been since your heart was overwhelmed with a sense of gratitude?

OFFERING THANKSGIVING IN PRAYER

As you use the Quiet Time section of your **Journal**, simply express the natural appreciation in your heart. To indicate your thanksgiving, write "T" in the margin as your code. Begin thanking God for the things in life which you may have taken for granted. Here are some practical examples:

	Scriptural Insight		Prayer
S A M P L E	m Titus 2:7 *"In all things show yourself to be an example of good deeds . . ."* The ministry of example may be the most important outreach I can have. vs. 2-3 Both older men and women are to live out the Christian faith in a way attractive to younger believers.	T	Lord, as I look back over the years I want to thank You for Sunday School teachers, friends and family members who have been good examples for me to follow.

Application:
I will write a thankyou note to Mrs. Dixon and let her know how much her life has meant to me. I will seek to make my own life a positive example to others.

☆	my meditation for today	A	Adoration
➜	further study needed	C	Confession
x	cross reference	T	Thanksgiving
m	verse(s) to memorize	P	Petition

4 PETITION
(Praying for Your Personal Needs)

"Until now you have asked for nothing in My name; ask, and you will receive, that your joy may be made full." (John 16:24, NAS)

On a day-to-day basis, most of your petitions will deal with small-scale problems, decisions and opportunities. That is natural, so don't consider your needs beneath God's interest. Remember, Jesus said the Father even knows when a sparrow falls!

Perhaps no verse in the New Testament is as helpful with regard to prayers of petition as John 14:13, in which Jesus said, *"And whatsoever ye shall ask in my name, that will I do, that the Father may be glorified in the Son."* (KJV)

In both large and small requests, the question should always be, "Is my prayer the kind that will *glorify* my heavenly Father?"

Pray about everything, and try not to confuse your *needs* with your *wants*. By faith, be prepared to *praise* Him for a *"yes"* or a *"no"* when He answers your petition. He knows your need, even before you ask. His promise is wonderfully understandable – *"Seek ye first the kingdom of God, and His righteousness; and all these things shall be added unto you."* (Matthew 6:33, KJV)

BRINGING PETITIONS TO GOD

As you learn to make your requests using the Quiet Time portion of your **Journal**, indicate your petitions with the symbol "P".

	Scriptural Insight		Prayer
S**A****M****P****L****E**	➤ Titus 1:7-9 The attributes for spiritual leadership are available to everyone, because they are character qualities that can be developed rather than human talents. This is good news!	P	Father, I want very much to have a godly character, so I can be used by You in ministry. Please prepare me for service any way, any time, anywhere.

Application:
This week I will ask Ruth Jones and Bill Smith what they did to develop the godly character which is so obvious in their lives.

☆	my meditation for today	A	Adoration
➤	further study needed	C	Confession
x	cross reference	T	Thanksgiving
m	verse(s) to memorize	P	Petition

5   INTERCESSION

(Praying for the Needs of Others)

". . . . far be it from me that I should sin against the Lord by ceasing to pray for you." (1 Samuel 12:23, NAS)

When Christ enters our lives, it becomes our spontaneous desire to seek God's blessings for those around us. This is called "intercession".

It would probably be safe to say that the most consistent intercessory praying which we do focuses on the spiritual needs of relative, friends and neighbours. Many of those we intercede for are lost. Others are Christians living beneath the resources and privileges freely available to God's children. In each of these instances, intercessory prayer is a ministry of love.

Through intercession, any Christian can be mightily used by God to affect the cause of evangelism worldwide. Whatever our physical condition, we can all be part of God's powerful army of prayer. Jesus said to His disciples, *"If you abide in Me, and My words abide in you, ask whatever you wish, and it shall be done for you."* (John 15:7, NAS)

INTERCEDING FOR OTHERS

List the names of *individuals* and *ministries* that you want to pray for. When possible, present their needs to God by name. Pray for them exactly as you would want them to pray for you.

The following pages provide for each day of the week. The example below shows how to use the code at the bottom of the Intercession pages:

	NAME	SPECIFIC REQUEST
S A M P L E	N John	Please show him what drinking will do to his life.
	F Dad	Give him wisdom in the job decision he is making.
	C Jim	Help him as he shares Christ with his grandmother.

F	Family	- immediate family and other relatives
M	Ministries	- church leaders, church services, missionaries and organizations
C	Close Friends	- relationships outside my immediate family
N	Non-Christian Friends	- those who have not yet come to know Christ
G	Government	- local and national officials and agencies

INTERCESSION

	NAME	SPECIFIC REQUEST
D A I L Y		
S U N D A Y		
M O N D A Y		
T U E S D A Y		

F	Family	- immediate family and other relatives
M	Ministries	- church leaders, church services, missionaries and organizations
C	Close Friends	- relationships outside my immediate family
N	Non-Christian Friends	- those who have not yet come to know Christ
G	Government	- local and national officials and agencies

INTERCESSION

	NAME	SPECIFIC REQUEST	
WEDNESDAY			*QUIET TIME*
THURSDAY			
FRIDAY			
SATURDAY			

F	Family	- immediate family and other relatives
M	Ministries	- church leaders, church services, missionaries and organizations
C	Close Friends	- relationships outside my immediate family
N	Non-Christian Friends	- those who have not yet come to know Christ
G	Government	- local and national officials and agencies

Scriptural Insights and Prayer

Scripture Memory Review	Date_____
	Memory Verse for the Week

S M T W T F S
☐ ☐ ☐ ☐ ☐ ☐ ☐

Scriptural Insight | Prayer

SUNDAY

Application:

MONDAY

Application:

TUESDAY

Application:

☆ my meditation for today	A Adoration
➤ further study needed	C Confession
x cross reference	T Thanksgiving
m verse(s) to memorize	P Petition

QUIET TIME

Week 1 ....

WEDNESDAY

Application:

THURSDAY

Application:

FRIDAY

Application:

SATURDAY

Application:

Scriptural Insights and Prayer

Scripture Memory Review	Date_____
_____	Memory Verse for the Week
_____	_____
_____	_____
_____	_____
S M T W T F S ☐ ☐ ☐ ☐ ☐ ☐ ☐	_____

	Scriptural Insight	Prayer
S U N D A Y		
	Application:	
M O N D A Y		
	Application:	
T U E S D A Y		
	Application:	

☆	my meditation for today	A	Adoration
➤	further study needed	C	Confession
x	cross reference	T	Thanksgiving
m	verse(s) to memorize	P	Petition

QUIET TIME

Week 2 ....

WEDNESDAY

Application:

THURSDAY

Application:

FRIDAY

Application:

SATURDAY

Application:

-15-

Scriptural Insights and Prayer

Scripture Memory Review	Date_____
_____	Memory Verse for the Week
_____	_____
_____	_____
S M T W T F S	_____
☐ ☐ ☐ ☐ ☐ ☐ ☐	_____

Scriptural Insight	Prayer

SUNDAY

Application:

MONDAY

Application:

TUESDAY

Application:

☆ my meditation for today	A Adoration
➤ further study needed	C Confession
x cross reference	T Thanksgiving
m verse(s) to memorize	P Petition

WEDNESDAY

Application:

THURSDAY

Application:

FRIDAY

Application:

SATURDAY

Application:

Scriptural Insights and Prayer

Scripture Memory Review	Date_____
	Memory Verse for the Week

S M T W T F S
☐ ☐ ☐ ☐ ☐ ☐ ☐

Scriptural Insight	Prayer

SUNDAY

Application:

MONDAY

Application:

TUESDAY

Application:

☆ my meditation for today	A Adoration
➤ further study needed	C Confession
x cross reference	T Thanksgiving
m verse(s) to memorize	P Petition

QUIET TIME

WEDNESDAY

Application:

THURSDAY

Application:

FRIDAY

Application:

SATURDAY

Application:

HOW TO USE THE NOTE TAKING SECTION

THIS SECTION CAN BE USED DURING:

Worship Services   **Group Bible Studies**
Evangelistic Meetings   **Conferences**

The **Journal's** approach to note taking is simplified through the use of symbols. When God impresses you with a thought during any part of a sermon, just write it down, code it, and continue note taking. After several weeks, you will become familiar with the symbols. At the end of each message, it will be easy to refer back to the subject areas which have been coded.

Explanation of Symbols:

☆ *Point to Remember:* This could be an outstanding quotation, a profound statement, or a new insight from God's Word.

➤ *Further Study Needed:* When you find a passage or thought of particular interest which you would like to study in more detail, code it with an "➤". If the word or passage is unclear, use the same code.

√ *Illustration:* Summarize good illustrations so you can remember them. You will find that the illustrations God uses to convict or challenge you will often communicate to others as well.

— *Cross Reference:* Many times a speaker will refer to related verses in the Bible. In each case, use an "—" to code those references. As you become increasingly acquainted with the Scriptures, God will begin bringing references to your mind as you listen to His Word.

○ *Application:* Applying God's Word is the most important principle in living the Christian life. To *emphasize* areas for application, code your notes with a circle, "○". Notice in the example how the application portions of the notes are circled, as well as coded. You will usually find it necessary to write out *specific steps* to put your application into immediate practice. Your applications need to be:

> PERSONAL: Select an activity *you* can do!
> SPECIFIC: Be *detailed* and *realistic*!
> MEASURABLE: Give yourself a *time limit*!

"Discipline yourself for the purpose of godliness" (1 Timothy 4:7b, NAS).

CODE		
☆ point to remember	Jan. 16	☑ Sermon
∨ illustration	*date*	☐ Bible Study
✕ cross reference	Rev. T. Jones — 1 John 5:11-12	☐ Book
➤ further study needed	*speaker* *text*	☐ Cassette Tape
○ personal application	Knowing God	☐ Other Meeting
	subject title	

". . . God has given us eternal life, and this life is in His Son" – v. 11

☆ To receive Christ is to begin an eternal relationship with God.

➤ "He who has the Son has life. He who does not have the Son of God does not have life." – v. 12.

○ Lord, I thank you for the eternal life that you have given me.

☆ All men are either saved or lost. There is no middle ground!

∨ Salvation resembles marriage. If I ask, "Are you married?" you would not answer, "I hope so", or "Perhaps". Only one of two answers could be correct: "Yes" or "No". The same is true with salvation. Either we have invited Jesus Christ into our hearts as Saviour, or we have not.

m Jesus said, "I am the way, the truth, and the life. No man comes unto the
x Father but by Me" (John 14:6). Christ is the only way to heaven!

The message of Christianity is unique. Jesus did not claim to be one prophet among many. He claimed to be the only Saviour. Because of His death on the cross on our behalf, we can choose to know God as our Father, rather than our judge.

☆ Every year millions of people die with no knowledge of Jesus Christ.

○ I need to develop a deeper burden for non-Christians.

○ This week I will talk to John Smith about what it means to be a Christian.

". . . Faith cometh by hearing . . ."

NOTE TAKING

CODE		
☆ point to remember	____date____	☐ Sermon
∨ illustration		☐ Bible Study
✕ cross reference	speaker _____ text	☐ Book
➤ further study needed		☐ Cassette Tape
○ personal application	subject title	☐ Other Meeting

" . . . Faith cometh by hearing . . . "

CODE
☆ point to remember
∨ illustration
✕ cross reference
➤ further study needed
○ personal application

_____ date _____ ☐ Sermon
                                   ☐ Bible Study
speaker _____ _____ text ☐ Book
                                   ☐ Cassette Tape
_____ subject title _____ ☐ Other Meeting

NOTE TAKING

". . . Faith cometh by hearing . . ."

CODE		
☆ point to remember	_____ date	☐ Sermon
V illustration		☐ Bible Study
✕ cross reference	speaker _____ text	☐ Book
➤ further study needed		☐ Cassette Tape
O personal application	_____ subject title	☐ Other Meeting

_____
_____
_____
_____
_____
_____
_____
_____
_____
_____
_____
_____
_____
_____
_____
_____
_____
_____
_____
_____
_____
_____
_____
_____
_____
_____
_____
_____
_____
_____
_____
_____
_____
_____
_____
_____
_____
_____

". . . Faith cometh by hearing . . ."

CODE		
☆ point to remember	date	☐ Sermon
∨ illustration		☐ Bible Study
✕ cross reference	speaker text	☐ Book
➤ further study needed		☐ Cassette Tape
○ personal application	subject title	☐ Other Meeting

NOTE TAKING

"... Faith cometh by hearing ..."

". . . Faith cometh by hearing . . ."

CHURCH FRIENDS LIST

Name	Address	Phone No.

NEXT ACT ON MY PART

l   letter
p   phone call
v   personal visit
o   other

ADDITIONAL AIDS

QUIET TIME HIGHLIGHTS

Date	Insight

MINISTRY GOALS AND ACTIVITIES
FOR THE MONTH OF _____

SUNDAY	MONDAY	TUESDAY	WEDNESDAY	THURSDAY	FRIDAY	SATURDAY